PATCHWORKBOOK

Easy Lessons for
Creative Quilt Design and Construction

JUDY MARTIN

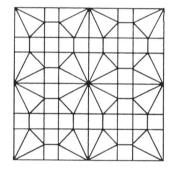

DOVER PUBLICATIONS, INC.

New York

To my husband, Steve Bennett

All the quilts illustrated in this book were made and designed by Judy Martin.
Photography by Birlauf and Steen Photo.

Design by Jennie Nichols/Levavi & Levavi

Published in Canada by General Publishing Company, Ltd., 30 Lesmill Road, Don Mills, Toronto, Ontario.
Published in the United Kingdom by Constable and Company, Ltd., 3 The Lanchesters, 162–164 Fulham Palace Road, London W6 9ER.

Bibliographical Note

This Dover edition, first published in 1993, is an unabridged republication of *Patchworkbook: Easy Lessons for Quilt Design and Construction*, first published by Charles Scribner's Sons, New York, in 1983.

Library of Congress Cataloging-in-Publication Data

Martin, Judy, 1950–
    Patchworkbook : easy lessons for creative quilt design and construction / Judy Martin.
       p.   cm.
    Originally published: New York : Scribner, 1983.
    Includes bibliographical references and index.
    ISBN 0-486-27844-1 (pbk.)
    1. Patchwork. 2. Quilting. I. Title.
[TT835.M38 1993]
746.9'7—dc20
                                                  93-32999
                                                    CIP

Manufactured in the United States of America
Dover Publications, Inc., 31 East 2nd Street, Mineola, N.Y. 11501

Acknowledgments

I would like to thank Marla Gibbs Stefanelli for helping me finish the artwork; Louise O. Townsend, Marie Shirer, and Linda Martin for proofreading, research, and editorial comments and suggestions; and Bonnie Leman for providing me with opportunities, experience, and a wonderful bunch of friends at *Quilter's Newsletter Magazine*.

Contents

Color Plates

Introduction

Patchworkbook is more than just another pattern book. Instead of presenting a handful of patterns, one or two of which you might eventually do, *Patchworkbook* gives you simple, step-by-step directions for creating your own original designs and for making the patterns yourself.

Why did I choose this approach? Over the years, designing original quilts has been gratifying for me, and through this book, I would like to help you experience for yourself the joys of creative quiltmaking.

Your original quilt design can be as adventuresome or as traditional as you like, but even if it looks like something that Martha Washington might have made, you will still have the pleasure of having made something uniquely yours and of contributing to America's quilt design legacy.

For inspiration, *Patchworkbook* shows you scores of new unit block and set designs and gives ideas for hundreds more. It teaches you everything that you need to know to design pieced quilts that can be drawn simply on graph paper. You don't have to be a wizard in geometry, and you won't need a compass, protractor, or other specialized drafting tools. Our method is easy enough for a beginner, but if you are an experienced quiltmaker and pattern drafter, you will find that you can use this approach to design quilts as intricate and challenging as you desire.

The easy format of lessons and exercises on every aspect of quilt design, planning, fabric selection, marking, cutting, and sewing makes *Patchworkbook* ideal for self-instruction or classroom use. The exercises are designed to give you practice in the skills you'll need to design and make your own quilt. Each one offers a "free play" section that you can repeat as often as you like and still find rewarding. The free play exercises provide a good review of the book and lead you step by step through the process of planning a quilt. In fact, you might want to go through these exercises each time that you try a design. The exercises should also remind you that this is not a coffee-table book or a book to keep on your shelf. It is a workbook. Write in it. Make notes. Color the pictures. And when you fill this book, start a loose-leaf notebook to keep the other great ideas and patterns that you'll surely continue to dream up.

Getting Started

American patchwork quilts are most often made of repeating patterned blocks arranged in rows. The basic repeating pattern is called the unit block. Unit blocks, in turn, are arranged into sets. The unit block and set approach to quiltmaking was recognized among America's pioneers as a boon to quiltmaking in cramped quarters. Unit blocks of manageable size could be made individually and joined later so that the problems of handling larger quilts could be avoided until the final stages of setting together the blocks.

For quiltmakers today, the use of unit blocks also simplifies the design process. You don't need a background in art to design original patchwork. Different combinations of blocks and sets provide countless design possibilities. Hundreds of traditional unit block patterns have been passed down through the generations and collected in many quilt books. Such blocks provide inspiration and a starting point from which to build your own designs. You can personalize the block design or simply arrange the traditional blocks in a new setting to create your original quilt design. You can work out your design in stages, starting with a single block, deciding on pattern, colors, and fabrics for that small area, and then plan the arrangement of your blocks in a set. Designing a quilt is not at all intimidating when it is approached in small steps. Even if you are a beginner, you can do it.

You will need these few basic tools for designing patchwork.

1. Graph Paper. I prefer fairly small squares—that is, ⅛″ squares (8 lines per inch) to ¹⁄₁₂″ squares (12 lines per inch) for designing patterns. The small squares permit you to work out more of the whole quilt design on one sheet of graph paper. Small squares also require fewer strokes when you are coloring, which saves time. For drafting patterns, you can use the same paper, simply ignoring the lines that you don't need. Some people prefer to draft the full-sized patterns on graph paper with ¼″ squares (4 lines per inch) because it is so easy to add ¼″ seam allowances to the pattern pieces that way. In fact, it is also easy to add seam allowances using 8-lines-per-inch paper or 12-lines-per-inch paper. For designing, graph paper need not be of the best quality, but for pattern drafting, get the best graph paper available. Lines should be straight, evenly spaced, and of uniform thickness. Graph paper of various rulings is available at stationery and engineering supply stores, college bookstores, some dime stores, and mail-order quilting supply sources.

2. Ruler. Accurate rulings and a straight edge are helpful. If you plan to do much pattern drafting, especially for machine piecing, you may find a clear plastic C-Thru® ruler a good investment. This ruler has the standard markings as well as a grid along its edge, which is handy for adding seam allowances to templates without measuring. C-Thru® rulers are available at stationery or office supply stores or where drafting equipment is sold. Some quilting and fabric stores also carry this or comparable rulers.

3. Tracing Paper (optional). When you are designing a quilt and want to experiment with different color schemes, you can save time by drawing the outline on graph paper and laying tracing paper over it to color the shapes without redrawing. This way, you can make several color versions from the same outline drawing. (If you have easy access to a photocopy machine, you can use it to reproduce your line drawing for color experimentation.)

4. Pencil with Eraser. A soft to medium-hard lead pencil (#2 to #3) is ideal for drawing block outlines. The eraser comes in handy for goofs or changes of mind.

5. Crayons, Colored Pencils, or Fiber-tip Pens in an Assortment of Colors. I like the vibrant colors and the manageability of fine-point fiber-tip pens. They make easy work of coloring either large areas or tiny spaces. Crayons can be used to fill in large areas, but they refuse to go where you aim them in small shapes. Colored pencils are good for small areas, but unless they are very soft, they make for slow going in large spaces. An advantage of colored pencils is that they permit you to grade the colors into any number of shades, depending on how hard you press. If you don't have a large selection of colors, you may find that the colored pencils permit more flexibility. Both fiber-tip pens and colored pencils are available in sets in art supply stores. However, you may prefer to augment the sets—or make up your own—with individual pens or pencils in several shades of just one or two color families. Don't expect to match your fabrics with the colored pens or pencils. Instead, use your color drawings to work out areas of contrast, subtle color gradations, and light or dark values. If you have a good selection of green pens, you can make your quilt drawing in greens, even if you plan to make your quilt from blue fabrics.

Once your tools are assembled, you're ready to begin. As you do the exercises in this book, you will train yourself to come up with all the ideas you'll ever need for designing original quilts.

ONE

Unit Blocks

The unit block is the small repeating pattern that is the basis of a quilt design. Study the photos on pages 27–30 and 119–126 to see how the quilts shown are made from unit blocks. On page 165 a single unit block is shown for each quilt to help you make sense of the pattern. Some quilt designs comprise more than one unit block; in these cases, each block is shown. A few of the designs are made in strips rather than from blocks. No blocks are shown for these. We'll discuss this kind of design after you have a thorough familiarity with unit blocks and sets.

Don't despair if you find it difficult to break down the quilt designs into blocks. While it's nice to be able to look at a quilt design and know at a glance how it is constructed, this isn't really a necessary skill for designing quilts. To design a quilt, you begin with the unit block and build a design from it. You will find that as you gain experience in designing quilts, your ability to recognize unit blocks will also improve.

Drawing Unit Blocks   1

Many traditional and original unit blocks are illustrated in this book. Each block has marks around the edges suggesting the graph grid on which the block would be drawn. You can easily copy any pattern onto your own graph paper as follows. Start by counting the number of squares needed for the block that you have chosen. If it helps you to see the relationship between the block and the graph grid, you can use a ruler and pencil to connect the marks around the block drawing with horizontal and vertical lines that form a grid over the design. (If you prefer not to write in the book, draw the grid on tracing paper over the block.) Count out the same number of squares on your graph paper, and outline this area. Each line within the block will begin and end at the corner of a graph square. Locate the starting and ending points for one of the lines in your pattern by counting how many squares to the left or right and up or down it is from the block outline. For example, the line might start at the top edge of the block, one square to the left of the right side. The same line might end at the bottom edge of the block, one square to the left of the right side. Find the corresponding points within the outlined area on your graph paper, and mark each with a dot. Connect the dots with a ruler and pencil line. Select another line, locate the starting and ending points for it, mark with dots, and connect the dots to make the line. It is easier to keep your bearings if you start with major lines, such as the ones that extend from edge to edge of the block. Continue marking dots and connecting them to make lines until the block is completed. Double check to make sure that you haven't missed any lines. Two examples of drawing blocks are shown on pages 3–4.

With practice, you will learn to identify on your own the number of squares needed to draw a pattern, enabling you to draw unit blocks from sources other than this book. If the block that you have chosen really has you stumped, attempt to draw it anyway. If your drawing fails to match the original, you may find that you have created an equally attractive new design.

To copy complicated patterns, you may find it helpful to start by measuring the block drawing and either the height or side dimension of the smallest patch in it. Divide the block size by the patch size. If the answer is a nice round number, that is probably the number of squares across the block. If the number is not so nice and round, it may be that the block does not lend itself to drawing on standard graph paper. Some blocks and quilt designs can be drawn only using compass, protractor, or special triangular, hexagonal, or diamond graph grids. A few examples are Grandmother's Flower Garden, Mariner's Compass, Drunkard's Path, and Lone Star.

If you haven't a clue as to how to draw the block, or if you suspect that your current skill level won't permit you to draw it, consider choosing another block. After all, with hundreds from which to choose, there must be another block that you like as well.

Study the unit blocks illustrated on pages 5–9. They are organized according to the number of squares needed to draw them on graph paper.

How to Draw Unit Blocks

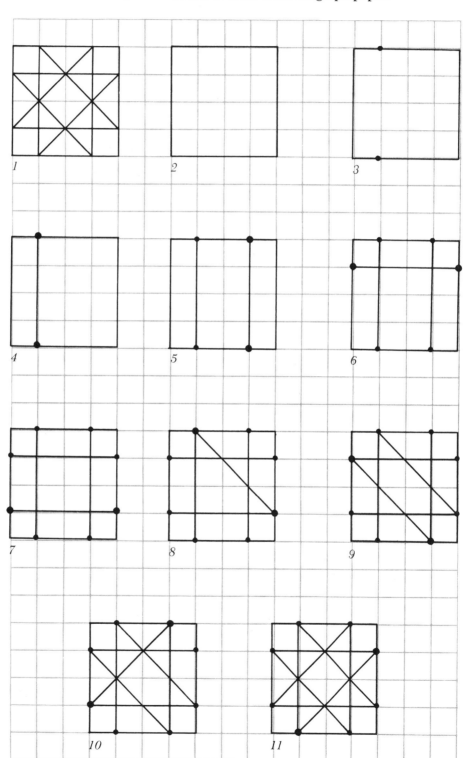

Left to right, top to bottom: (1) *Select a unit block—this one is Variable Star—and determine how many squares are needed to draw it. Draw horizontal and vertical lines connecting the marks around the edges, if you like.* (2) *Outline a corresponding number of squares on your graph paper.* (3) *Choose a major line, locate the starting and ending points, and mark with dots.* (4) *Connect the dots to make a line.* (5–11) *Continue line by line, locating starting and ending points, marking with dots, and connecting dots until the block is complete.*

How to Draw Unit Blocks

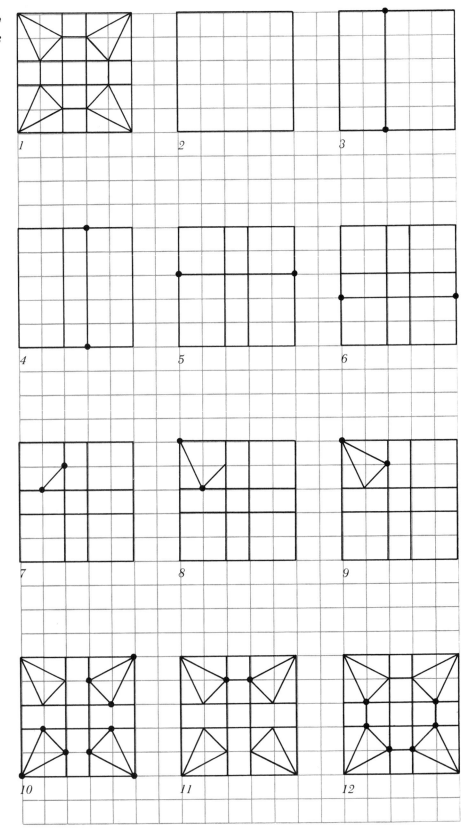

Left to right, top to bottom: (1) *Select a block—this one is Piñata—and determine how many graph squares are needed to draw it.* (2) *Outline a corresponding number of squares on your graph paper.* (3) *Choose a major line, locate starting and ending points, mark with dots, and connect dots to make line.* (4–12) *Continue marking and adding lines, first filling in one corner, then the others, until the block is complete.*

Unit Blocks Based on Grid of 4 × 4 Squares

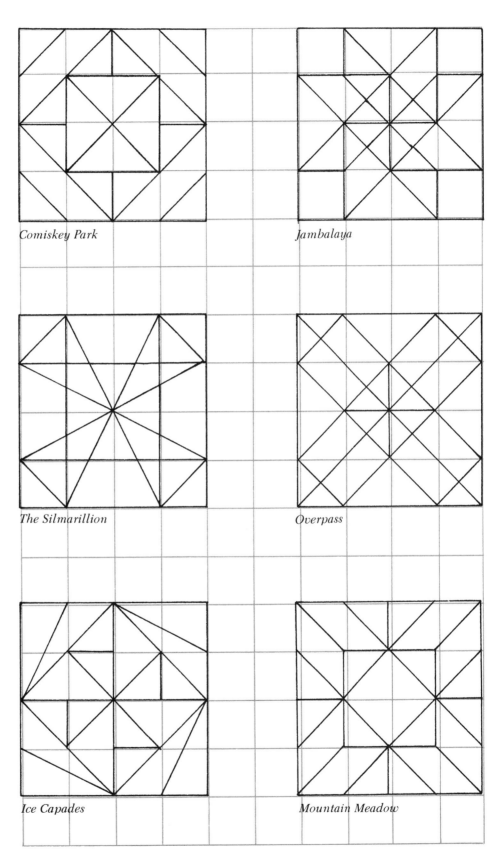

Comiskey Park

Jambalaya

The Silmarillion

Overpass

Ice Capades

Mountain Meadow

**Unit Blocks Based
on Grid of 5 × 5
Squares**

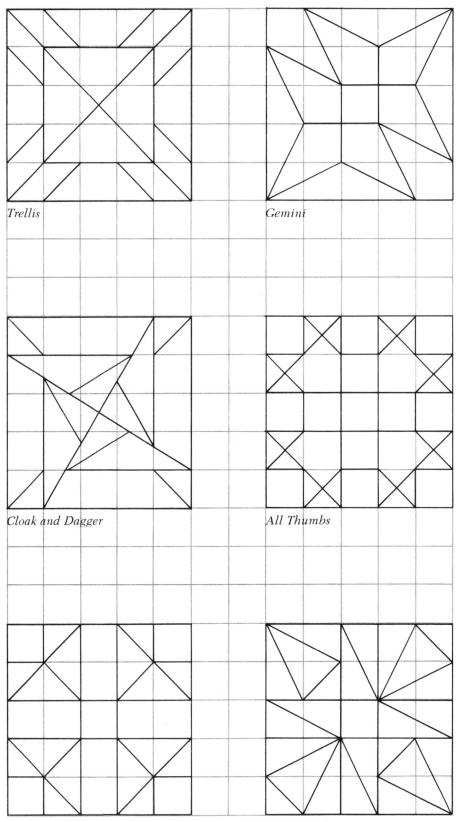

Trellis

Gemini

Cloak and Dagger

All Thumbs

Paper Airplanes

Cheerleaders

Unit Blocks Based on Grid of 6 × 6 Squares

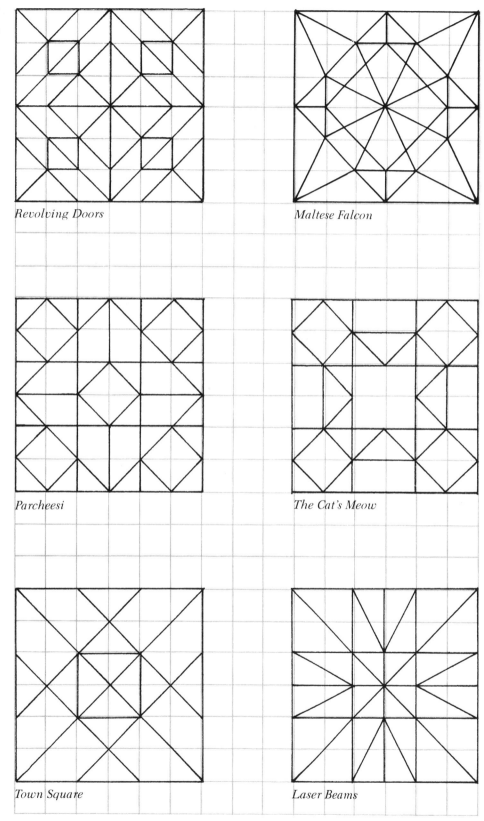

Revolving Doors

Maltese Falcon

Parcheesi

The Cat's Meow

Town Square

Laser Beams

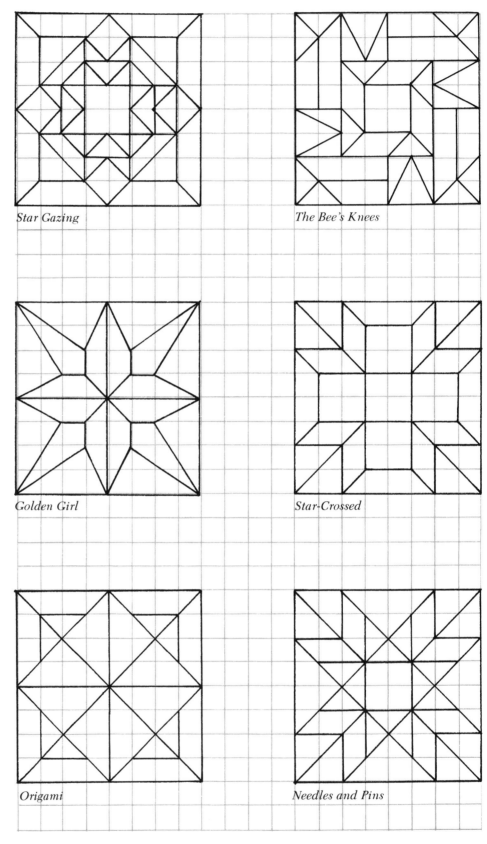

Star Gazing

The Bee's Knees

Golden Girl

Star-Crossed

Origami

Needles and Pins

Unit Blocks Based on Grid of 10 × 10 Squares

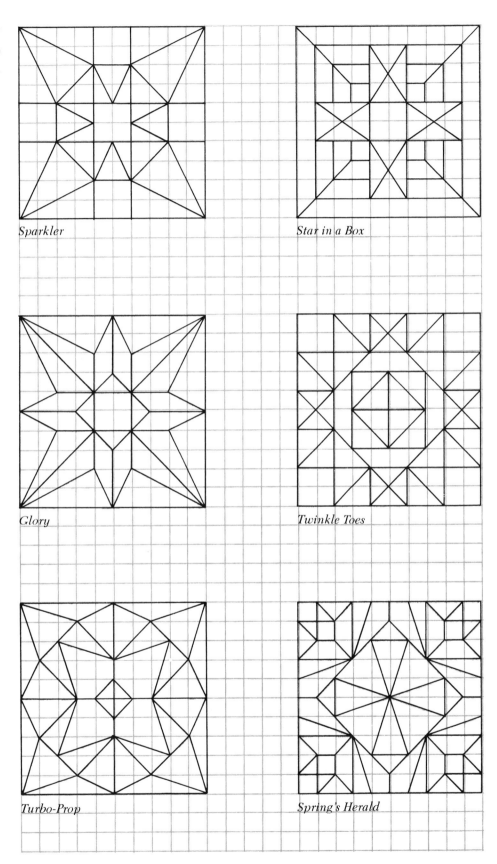

Sparkler

Star in a Box

Glory

Twinkle Toes

Turbo-Prop

Spring's Herald

EXERCISE

DRAWING THE UNIT BLOCK

A. Complete the unit block drawings at the right to match the drawings shown to the left of them. Mark starting and ending points for each line, and connect the dots with lines.

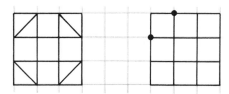

Shoo Fly

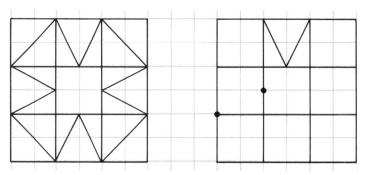

The Eight-Pointed Star

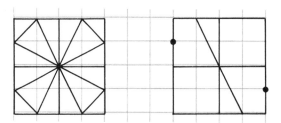

Connecticut

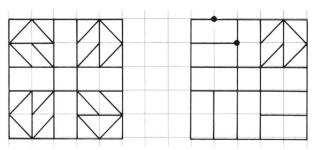

Whirligig

B. Draw the unit blocks shown. A suitable square is outlined on the graph grid next to each block. Mark starting and ending points for each line (beginning with the major ones), connect the dots, and continue until the block is completed.

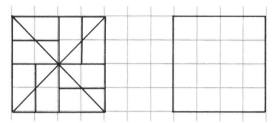

Tutti-Frutti

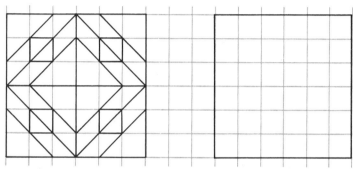

Star Tracks

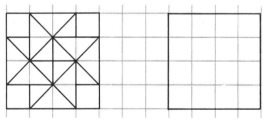

Gypsy

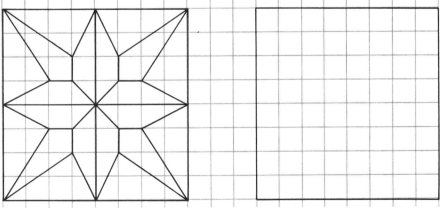

Golden Girl

C. Copy the unit blocks shown onto your own graph paper. Start by counting the number of squares across and down the example, and outlining a corresponding area on your graph grid. (Suggestion: If you find it helpful, you can connect the marks around the edges of the blocks here to form a grid over the blocks.)

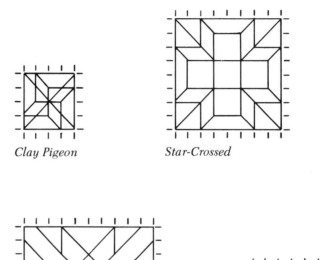

Clay Pigeon   *Star-Crossed*

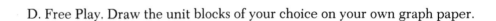

Mexican Star   *Path and Stiles*

D. Free Play. Draw the unit blocks of your choice on your own graph paper.

TWO

Block Variations

Now that you are familiar with a number of unit blocks and know how to draw them, let's explore the ways of personalizing unit blocks. With a little imagination, you should be able to adapt a standard unit block to make something uniquely yours.

Here are four properties of the unit block that you can change to create your own original design:

    1. Pattern   3. Proportions
    2. Coloring   4. Orientation

Let's take a look at these variables one at a time, and see how you can manipulate them to create new designs.

Block Pattern

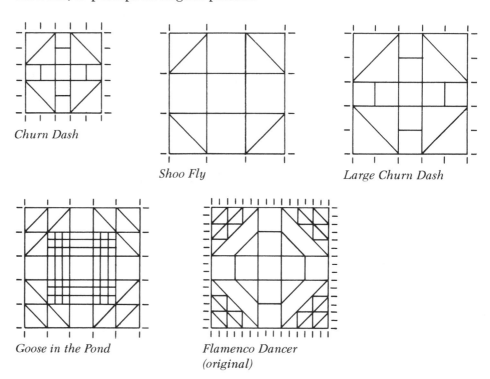

The single most important property of a unit block is its pattern. By pattern, I mean the arrangement of shapes in the block. In an outline drawing of a block, as shown in this book, the pattern is the arrangement of *lines* within the block. You distinguish a Churn Dash block from a Shoo Fly block by its pattern. If you change the color or size of a Churn Dash, you still have a Churn Dash. If you change the pattern, though, by changing the lines or arrangement of shapes, you no longer have a Churn Dash. Instead, you will have a Shoo Fly, a Goose in the Pond, or perhaps an original pattern.

Churn Dash

Shoo Fly

Large Churn Dash

Goose in the Pond

Flamenco Dancer (original)

With so many blocks from which to choose, the selection of a pattern has always been one of the more creative parts of planning and making a quilt. By changing the detail of a traditional pattern, you can be even more creative. Change a pattern just a little bit, perhaps to add a shape that will show off a special fabric that you plan to use. Or, if you like, use the traditional block simply as a starting point for designing an original block that scarcely resembles the source block.

You can personalize a pattern by adding or subtracting lines, or by doing a little of both. Simply draw the unit block in pencil on graph paper. Leave it in

14

bare outline form, not colored in. Then add lines or erase lines to create your own unique design. Some of the designs that you derive are bound to duplicate traditional patterns. Others, though, will be truly original.

Adding Lines

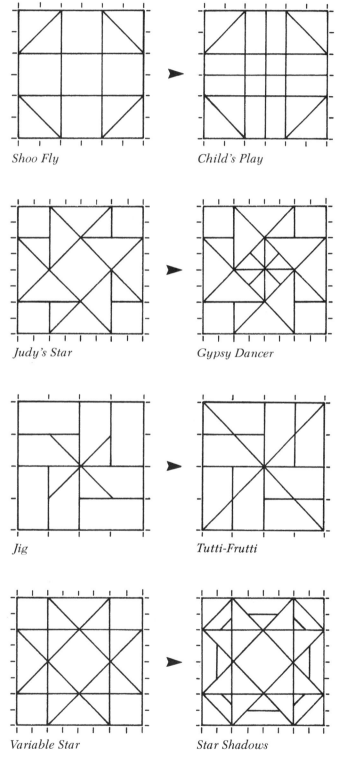

Shoo Fly

Child's Play

Judy's Star

Gypsy Dancer

Jig

Tutti-Frutti

Variable Star

Star Shadows

Subtracting Lines

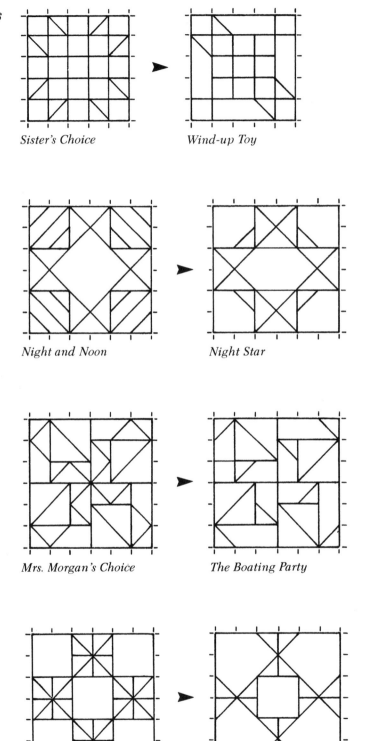

Sister's Choice

Wind-up Toy

Night and Noon

Night Star

Mrs. Morgan's Choice

The Boating Party

Four-Leaf Clover

Arapahoe

*Adding and
Subtracting Lines*

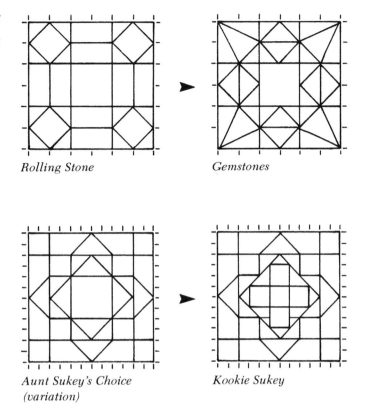

Rolling Stone   Gemstones

Aunt Sukey's Choice   Kookie Sukey
(variation)

When you are adding detail to a block pattern, you may want to simply rough in the new lines on your first block drawing. If you come up with an embellishment that you like, study your rough drawing. Have you added any lines that fall *between* graph lines rather than *on* the graph lines? If your new block has lines that are halfway between graph lines, redraw the pattern on a grid containing twice as many squares across the block (and twice as many squares down). For each square on the original drawing, count two squares on the new drawing (and for each half-square on the original, count one square on the new drawing). By doing this, you can draw your new pattern with complete accuracy. Similarly, if your new pattern has any lines dividing a graph square in thirds, redraw the pattern on a grid having three times the original number of graph squares across the block (and down the block).

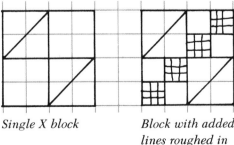

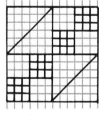

Single X block   Block with added   Jacob's Nine-Patch,
                        lines roughed in   new block
                                                   redrafted perfectly

When you add lines or erase them from the block drawing, you must keep in mind the limitations of construction. Try to avoid adding lines or removing lines in ways that make the construction of the block difficult. An unrealistically large number of pieces, many seams coming together in one place, and awkward shapes that could more easily be made from more than one patch are some of the things that you should avoid.

Figs. 1–3: *Avoid too many narrow points coming together in one place when adding lines to a block. Fig. 1 is a source block, Beautiful Dreamer. Fig. 2 shows a new block derived from it. This single block might not be unrealistic, but if you plan to set the blocks side by side, as in Fig. 3, sixteen narrow points come together at each corner where four blocks meet. The sewing becomes quite tricky here.*

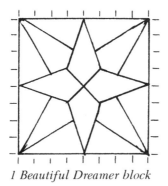

1 Beautiful Dreamer block

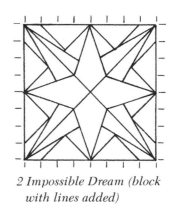

2 Impossible Dream (block with lines added)

3 Four Impossible Dream blocks set together

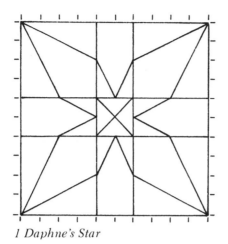

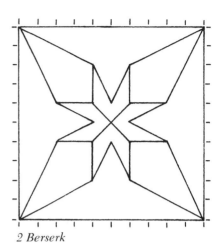

1 Daphne's Star

2 Berserk

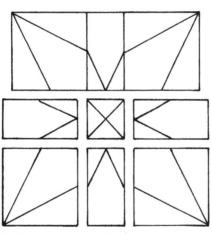

Figs. 1–4: *Avoid awkward shapes when subtracting lines, and don't remove lines that are needed for reasonable construction. Fig. 1 shows a source block, Daphne's Star. Fig. 2 shows Berserk, a proposed block derived by subtracting lines from it. Fig. 3 shows how Daphne's Star would be constructed from rows. Fig. 4 shows the difficult construction that would be involved in making Berserk.*

3 Construction of Daphne's Star

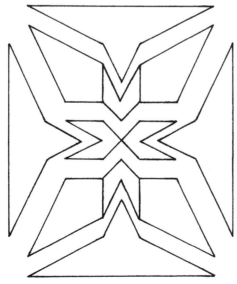

4 Construction of Berserk

Study the unit blocks throughout the book to become familiar with the range of pattern possibilities. Notice the basic divisions of blocks into thirds or fifths or halves. Notice how the dividing lines cut the blocks vertically and horizontally or diagonally. Make yourself aware of interesting corner treatments or ways of embellishing a center square. If you keep in mind some of these block features, you will be able to use them in new combinations to create original patterns. Putting together the elements of different unit blocks provides an excellent source of ideas for changing the pattern detail. The illustrations below show a few examples.

Combining Elements of Different Blocks

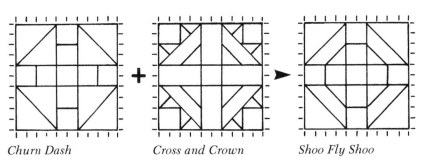

Churn Dash   *Cross and Crown*   *Shoo Fly Shoo*

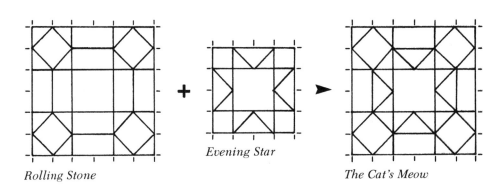

Rolling Stone   *Evening Star*   *The Cat's Meow*

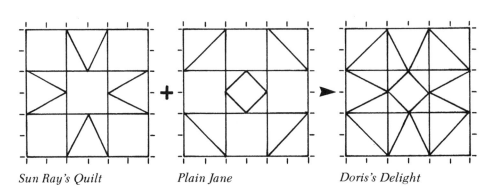

Sun Ray's Quilt   *Plain Jane*   *Doris's Delight*

EXERCISE

CHANGING THE PATTERN IN THE BLOCK

A. Adding Lines. Create your own variations of the patterns shown by copying the blocks onto your own graph paper and adding lines to make new patterns. If your new pattern has lines that fall between lines on your graph grid, redraw it on your graph paper. Use twice as many squares across and down, or three times as many, or whatever number of squares will allow you to draw the new pattern accurately.

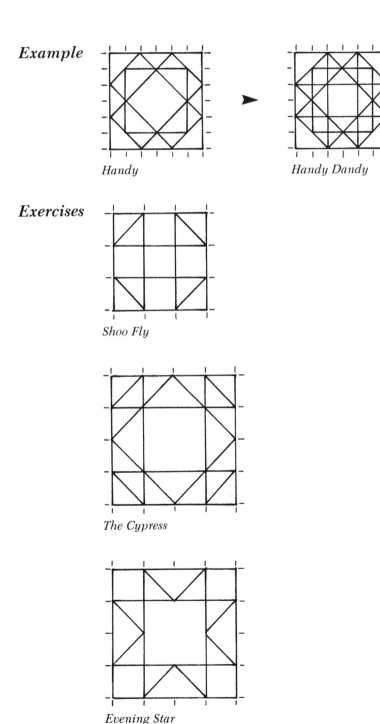

Example

Handy　　　　　　　*Handy Dandy*

Exercises

Shoo Fly

The Cypress

Evening Star

B. Subtracting Lines. Copy the following unit blocks in pencil onto your own graph paper. As you draw, notice the pattern developing. You may see a design that you like in the partially completed drawing. If so, stop there. Otherwise, continue drawing until the block is completed. Then erase selected lines to change the pattern. Do not erase lines that are necessary for construction of the unit block.

Example

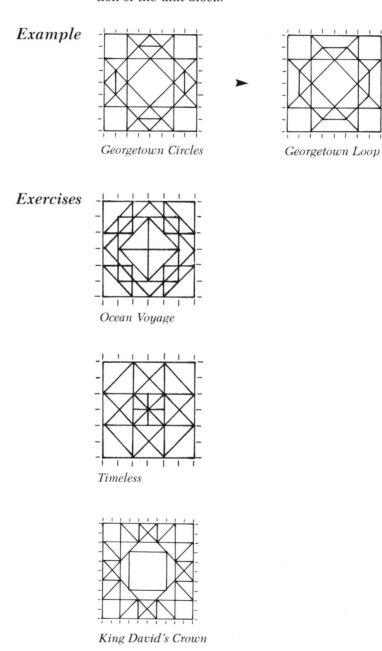

Georgetown Circles

Georgetown Loop

Exercises

Ocean Voyage

Timeless

King David's Crown

C. Free Play. Repeat Exercise A or B, copying the unit block of your choice onto graph paper and adding or subtracting lines. Consider the possibility of combining elements of two blocks.

Block Coloring 3

One of the pleasures of quiltmaking is choosing the colors. The selection of colors offers much room for self-expression. Even with the few patterns such as Corn and Beans, Storm at Sea, or Burgoyne Surrounded that are traditionally made in specific colors, you can select the particular shade of color and the nature of the prints to suit your own taste. The vast majority of the unit block patterns do not have traditional color schemes (and even those that do are not above variation). You are free, then, to personalize the unit block by choosing your own colors and materials.

You can use color to achieve strong contrast or subtle gradation. You can use bright or dark colors in the background for emphasis, or you can get a completely different effect by using a light or neutral background that fades back. Here are a few examples showing the effect of substituting one color for another.

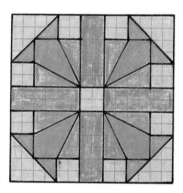

Figs. 1–4 show the Bluebell block in various colors.

1

2

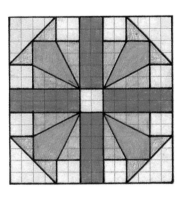

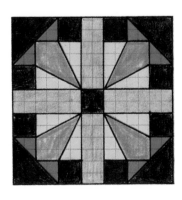

3

4

Even greater variation is possible if you change the placement of colors within the block in order to highlight different parts of the pattern. To do this, first you must consider the pattern as a bare outline. Then you group the pieces in a new relationship (different from the traditional coloring), using the color arrangement to bring some elements together and to isolate others. Shapes that are colored the same will be seen as a unit. By your placement of colors, you can bring out a star shape—or you can play down the star and emphasize a grouping of squares, instead. You can color the block asymmetrically, with two corners matching and the other two different. Every block has a number of coloring possibilities. You can change the arrangement of colors in the block without ever changing the color scheme. Notice how the examples in the illustrations that follow use the same colors in different arrangements to change the appearance of the patterns.

Figs. 1–2 show Rambler colored two ways.

1

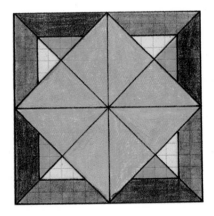

2

Figs. 3–4 show Origami colored asymmetrically and symmetrically.

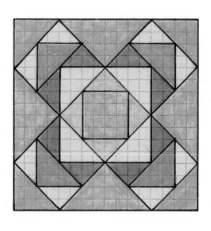

3

4

EXERCISE

CHANGING THE COLORING IN THE BLOCK

A. Experiment with different color schemes. Color the first block of each pair, then substitute one color for another when you color the second block. See what different effects you can achieve in each pair of blocks. (Suggestion: Try using light vs. dark backgrounds or strong vs. subtle color differences.)

Example

 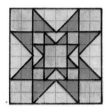

Rising Star   *Rising Star*

Exercises

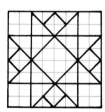 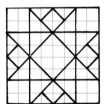

Greengrocer's Tile

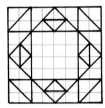 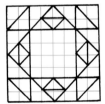

Grandmother's Favorite

B. Use different placement of colors in the pairs of blocks given to achieve different effects. Color the first block of each pair to bring together certain parts of the design; color the second block to bring together other shapes. (Suggestion: Try coloring a block asymmetrically, with two corners different from the other two.)

Example

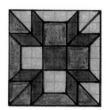

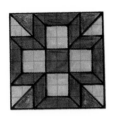

Star-Crossed   *Star-Crossed*

Exercises

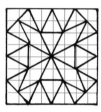

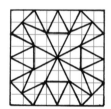

Icing on the Cake

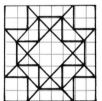

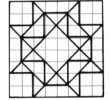

Snowball Stars

C. Free Play. Copy a unit block of your choice onto graph paper, and experiment with coloring as suggested in Exercises A and B to create a pleasing design.

1. STAR GAZING   1981   63″ × 73″ The unit block is an original one combining an embellishment of the basic traditional Evening Star with the format of another original block, Origami. The blocks were set side by side to form cross shapes between them. These crosses were continued into the border, as were the small white squares. Other shapes were added to fill in the border space between these patches. For definition, the outer edge of the border was made from darks and brights only, with the white eliminated.

2. NINE-PATCH VARIATION 1978 103″ × 103″ The unit block is a simple Nine Patch split in half along the diagonal. One half of the block was made of light scraps, the other half darker. The 256 small blocks were colored in a multitude of combinations to create the overall pattern of zigzagging concentric bands. The quilt plan was colored as a whole, ignoring the unit blocks. The change of colors, with the darkest band on the outside, simulates a border. The scrap prints were carefully chosen for the graded color bands, but the variability of prints within each band makes the quilt dance and shimmer.

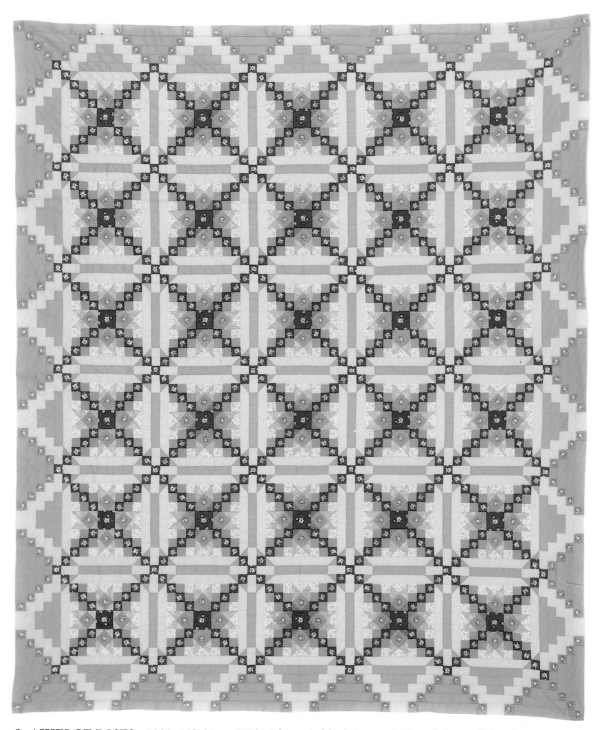

3. ASHES OF ROSES   1980   76¼″ × 86⅝″ The unit block is a variation of the traditional pattern
Stepping Stones. The pattern detail was changed slightly to incorporate the pink square turned on point,
which shows off a printed motif to advantage. The block size was adjusted to fit the squares to the floral
prints. The coloring was changed to resemble a Double Irish Chain pattern.

The quilt blocks were set together with pieced sashing that was inspired by an obscure Nancy Cabot
quilt *block* pattern called Garden Paths. The arrangement of setting squares and sashing accentuates the
strong diagonal movement of the quilt by permitting the chains of flowers cut from the dark print to
march across the quilt uninterrupted. The pale, solid-colored sashing strips provide some relief from the
prints in the blocks. They also provide some horizontal and vertical lines to balance the strong diagonals.
Because of their soft color and angular shape, the sashing strips do not box in the quilt blocks too much.

The squares crossing the quilt continue into the borders, but the color is softened. The pattern in the
borders is simplified to just these squares and pale green rectangles, like the ones in the pieced sashing,
echoing the squares. Darker green rectangles fill in the remaining space in the borders. The color
concentration and use of prints and solids change in the borders to give the quilt definition around the
perimeter.

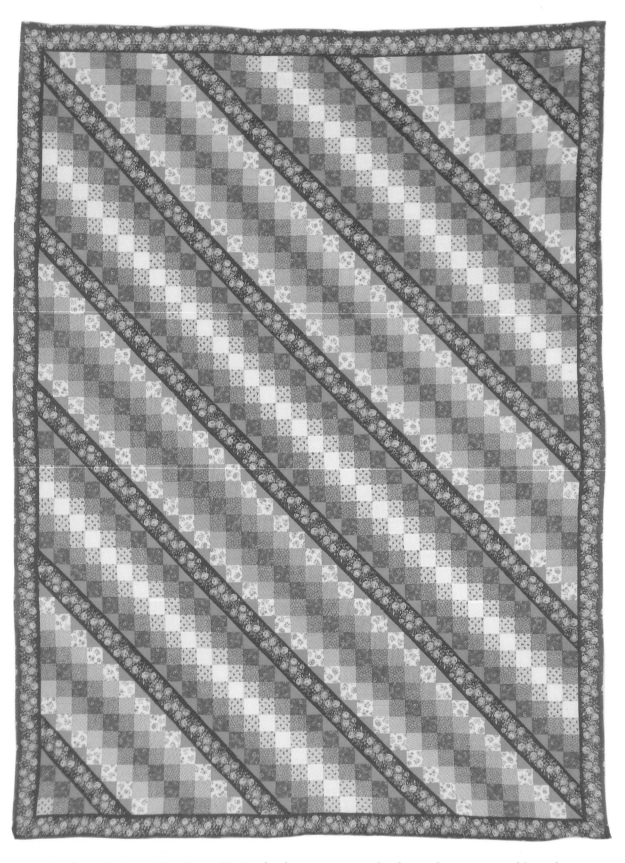

4. ANGEL'S FLIGHT   1979   65″ × 85″ Bands of squares, set on the diagonal, are separated by sashing in one direction only. The quilt was made strippie style, in rows without blocks. A floral stripe adds interest in this simple design.

Block Proportions 4

Changing proportions in the block involves enlarging or reducing different parts of the block by different amounts. You can make the center smaller and the corners larger, or you can do just the opposite. You can make one corner small and the opposite corner large or the whole top edge small and the bottom edge large. The change can be obvious or subtle, and it can affect the overall pattern of the quilt as well as the character of the individual block. The change of proportions can produce some traditional-looking variations, or it can yield some unusual and dramatic asymmetrical designs, according to your taste. Here are some traditional blocks and variations derived from changing proportions.

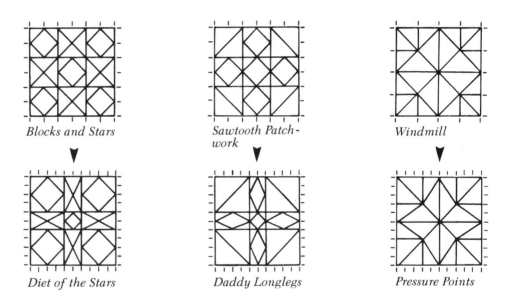

Blocks and Stars *Sawtooth Patch-work* *Windmill*

Diet of the Stars *Daddy Longlegs* *Pressure Points*

In order to change the proportions of the blocks, simply redraw the design on a grid of squares and rectangles, rather than the usual grid of identical squares. Start by picturing the graph grid on which the traditional block would be drawn. The Variable Star (see page 32) would be drawn on a graph grid of 4 × 4 squares, as shown. Instead of using the usual 4 × 4 grid, draw a substitute grid on graph paper, using more than 4 × 4 graph squares to make four rows and four columns of varying widths. Several possible grids for 4 × 4 blocks are shown in the six grids below the Variable Star. Note that the new block format may be symmetrical or asymmetrical, square or rectangular.

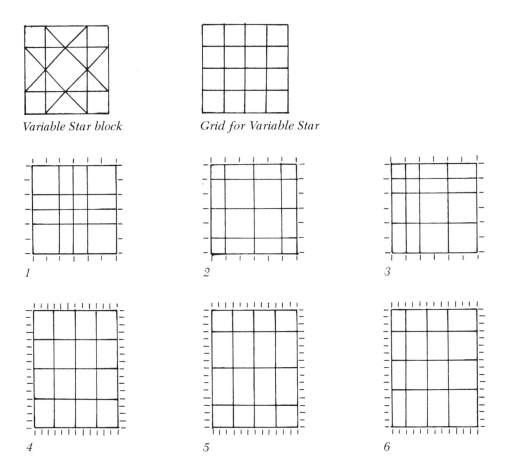

Variable Star block   *Grid for Variable Star*

Figs. 1–6 show several possible grids for 4 × 4 blocks.

Finally, draw your block design on the new grid. Proceed as usual, locating starting and ending points of lines to correspond with those on the source block (the Variable Star in our example). Ignore printed graph lines that fall *between* the drawn lines of your new grid when locating points. Mark with dots, and connect the dots with pencil and ruler to draw the lines. The two examples below show the first few lines of the Variable Star block being drawn on a new grid.

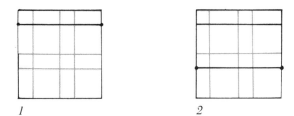

For diagonal lines, you will need to mark intermediate points as well as starting and ending points. Mark points to correspond to each place where a line crosses a corner of a graph square on the source block. For example, in the source pattern, a line may run diagonally through three graph squares, as in Fig. 1 on page 33. (This occurs in the Variable Star example.) Instead of drawing a simple straight line between the corresponding starting and ending points on your new grid, as in the second figure, draw three short lines from corner to corner of the three squares or rectangles that correspond to the three squares of the source block. The correct way to do this is shown in Fig. 3 in this sequence.

1

2 Wrong way
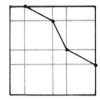
3 Right way

Here are six examples of the Variable Star block drawn on the grids shown in the illustrations on page 32. Note the great variety of patterns possible when you change block proportions.

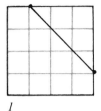
1
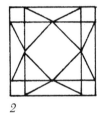
2
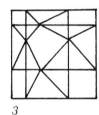
3

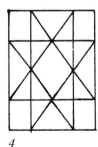
4
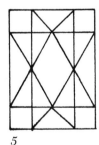
5
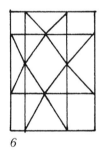
6

Here are several more examples of original blocks derived from traditional patterns, but with proportions changed by drawing the blocks on revised grids, as shown.

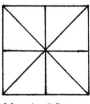
Mosaic #9

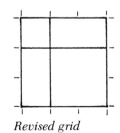
Revised grid

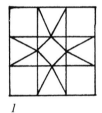
*Compressed
Pinwheel*

Mosaic #2

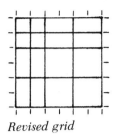

Revised grid

Variation

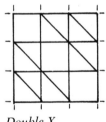

Swing in the Center

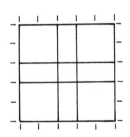

Revised grid

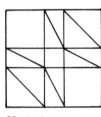

Variation

EXERCISE

CHANGING PROPORTIONS IN THE BLOCK

A. Copy the following blocks onto the grids provided. Begin by locating the starting and ending points as well as intermediate points at intersections of grid lines. Then mark with dots, and connect to make the lines of the new block.

Example

Double X

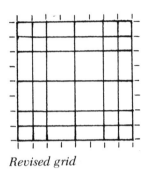

Revised grid

Variation

Exercises

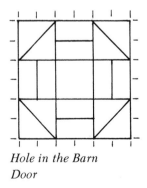

Hole in the Barn Door

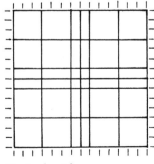

Revised grid

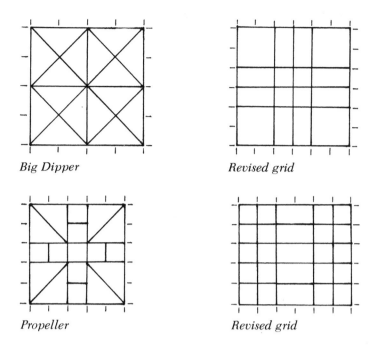

Big Dipper   *Revised grid*

Propeller   *Revised grid*

B. Change proportions in the following blocks by drawing a new grid for each on your own graph paper and proceeding to draw the block on the new grid. Remember that the new grid must contain more *graph* squares than the usual grid for the block shown, without changing the number of *rows* of squares and rectangles.

Example

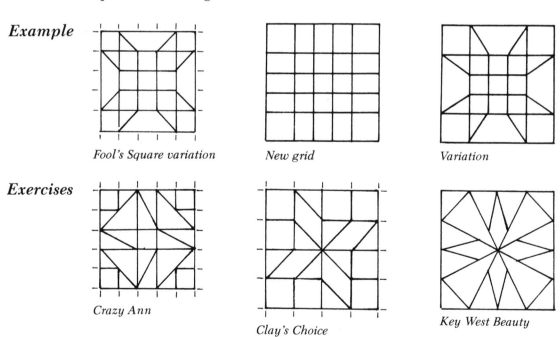

Fool's Square variation   *New grid*   *Variation*

Exercises

Crazy Ann

Clay's Choice

Key West Beauty

C. Free Play. Select a unit block of your choice, draw a revised grid for it on graph paper, and copy the block onto the new grid to create an original block design.

Block Orientation 5

When I talk about the orientation of a unit block, I am talking about which end is up or which way the block is tipped or turned. Most blocks are symmetrical—they are the same on all four sides. A symmetrical block will look the same no matter which side is on top. You *can* change the appearance of the block, though, by turning it on the diagonal, so that the corner, rather than the straight side, is on top.

When you are drawing an individual unit block, the orientation is not really a consideration. You can draw the pattern in the ordinary way and then simply turn the paper to change the orientation. If you like the way the block looks when you turn the paper, you may want to alter the block so that the design is turned on end when the block is set straight on its base side. Here are some examples showing traditional blocks and blocks with the designs turned on end.

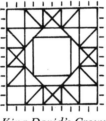

King David's Crown

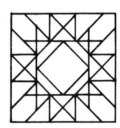

Variation

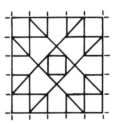

Providence block

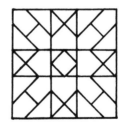

Road to Providence

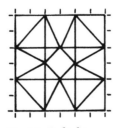

Doris's Delight

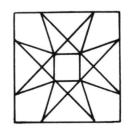

The Electronic Age

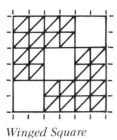

Winged Square

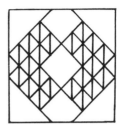

Winged Diamond

Follow this procedure to change the orientation of the design within the block. Draw the unit block in pencil on graph paper, leaving off or erasing the block outline. Next, draw a new block outline on the diagonal by connecting points on the edges of the design and crossing from corner to corner of the graph squares. Your new outline may cut through unimportant parts of the pattern. If necessary, extend the original lines to touch the new block outline. The following illustrations demonstrate this procedure. Note that the resulting block drawing is turned corner up on the graph paper.

Changing the Orientation of the Design in the Block by Making New Block Outlines on the Diagonal

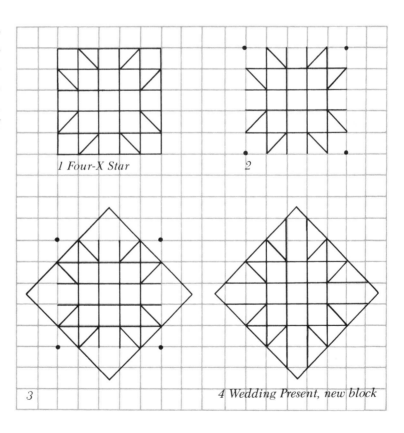

1 Four-X Star   2

3   4 Wedding Present, new block

Fig. 1. Traditional block. Fig. 2. Block copied with block outlines eliminated (dots indicate former block corners). Fig. 3. New block outlines drawn, connecting points at edges of block and crossing from corner to corner of graph squares. Fig. 4. Lines extended inside new block to meet outlines.

For a different effect, you can eliminate the block outline, and draw a new outline not exactly on the diagonal, but skewed somewhat off the true diagonal. Be careful to make your new outline form a square, with right angles in the corners and sides of equal length. The figures below show this procedure.

Unit Block Changed with Design Skewed

Fig. 1. Traditional unit block. Fig. 2. Unit block copied with block outlines eliminated (dots indicate former corners of block). Fig. 3. Ruler is aligned with points of triangles at block edges, and new block outlines are drawn. Fig. 4. Lines extending past the new block outlines are erased to complete block.

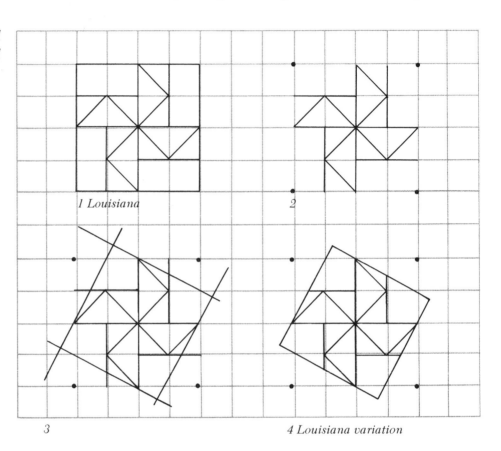

1 *Louisiana*

2

3

4 *Louisiana variation*

EXERCISE

CHANGING ORIENTATION IN THE BLOCK

A. Copy the following blocks, eliminating the outer boundaries. Then add new block outlines on the diagonal. (The first two are started for you.) The diagonal lines around the block should connect the points or lines at the edge of the block design. Extend other lines, as needed, to meet the new block outlines.

Example

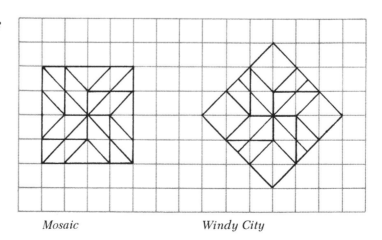

Mosaic   *Windy City*

Exercises

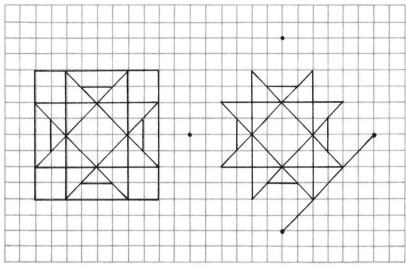

Edinburgh Star

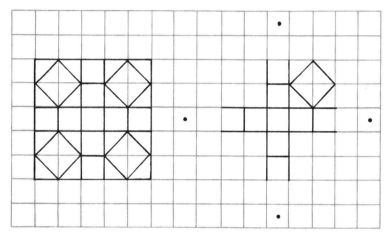

Rolling Stone

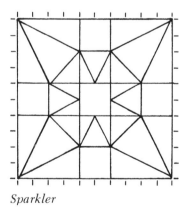

Sparkler

B. Copy the blocks on page 40, eliminating the block outlines and adding new ones that are skewed slightly off the true diagonal. Extend or erase original pattern lines so that they meet the new block boundaries. (The first two are started for you.)

Example

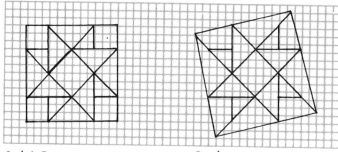

Judy's Star   *Starlet*

Exercises

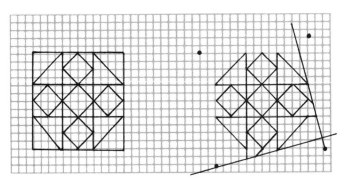

Sawtooth Patchwork

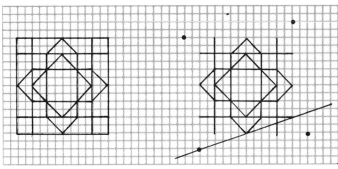

Aunt Sukey's Choice
(variation)

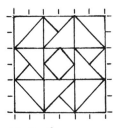

Air Castle

C. Free Play. On graph paper, copy the unit block of your choice, and eliminate the block outline. Add a new outline on the diagonal as in Exercise A or slightly skewed as in Exercise B. Extend lines to meet the new boundaries of the block, or erase extensions beyond the new outlines.

THREE

Sets

Now that you have experimented with unit blocks, you are no doubt anxious to use your new block ideas in a quilt design. There are many different ways to put the blocks together in your quilt. The arrangement of unit blocks is called the set. These are the three basic ways of putting together sets:

1. Adjacent Unit Blocks
2. Alternating Plain Blocks
3. Sashed Blocks

Basic Sets

6

Adjacent Unit Blocks. In this set, unit blocks are simply placed side by side in an overall pattern. The unit blocks appear to run together in this set, and the interaction of adjacent blocks can yield some interesting effects not apparent in the single unit block. In the first illustration the Piñata block is shown in a set of adjacent unit blocks.

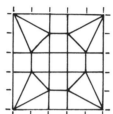

Piñata block

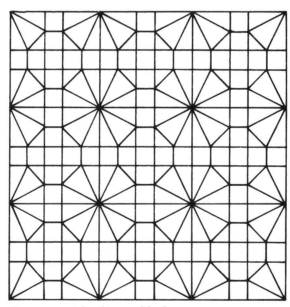

Piñata set with adjacent blocks

Alternating Plain Blocks. Here, the unit blocks are set together with plain blocks of the same size between them. The plain blocks and the unit blocks are arranged in checkerboard fashion over the quilt surface. In this arrangement, the interaction of the unit blocks is not as strong as it is in adjacent unit block sets. There is, however, some interaction where the pieced blocks touch. The plain blocks provide an ideal space to show off fine quilting. The illustration on page 43 shows a set with alternate plain blocks.

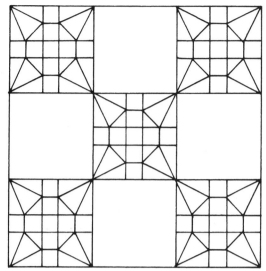

Piñata set with alternate plain blocks

Sashed Blocks. Here, the unit blocks are set together with strips between them. The strips define the boundaries of the individual blocks and give a very orderly appearance to the quilt. Sashing strips tend to isolate the unit blocks, minimizing the interplay between neighboring blocks. For this reason, sashing is usually more effective when used with unit blocks that can stand alone, such as the various star blocks, than with blocks that must be set side by side to make the design complete. The illustration below shows blocks set with sashing.

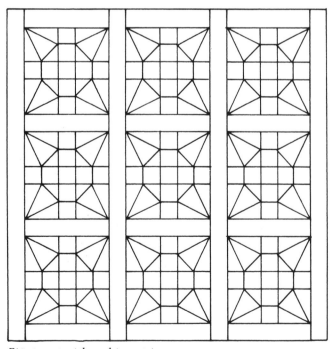

Piñata set with sashing strips

The choice of adjacent, sashed, or alternating plain blocks is one of the most important quilt design variables. The pattern of the unit block itself should suggest which of the basic sets is most suitable. Blocks that are uninteresting alone may improve when set next to each other. Blocks that stand alone well, especially detailed ones, might be set alternately with plain blocks which offer some relief from a busy pattern. Blocks like Shoo Fly, Four-X Star, or Rolling Stone (shown in the following illustrations) might call for a sashed arrangement that echoes the block's basic organization around intersecting center strips.

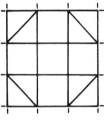

Shoo Fly

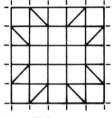

Four-X Star

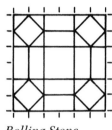

Rolling Stone

EXERCISE

THE THREE BASIC SETS

Example

A. Adjacent Unit Blocks. On your own graph paper, draw each of the following blocks in an adjacent block set. Draw at least three rows of three blocks side by side to establish the pattern.

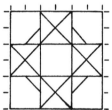 *Baseball Star block*

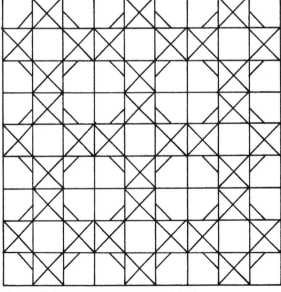

Baseball Star set with adjacent blocks

Exercises

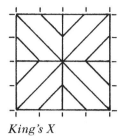

King's X

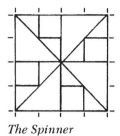

The Spinner

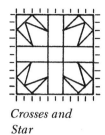

Crosses and
Star

B. Alternating Plain Blocks. Draw each of the following unit blocks in a set with alternating plain blocks. In the first row, draw two pieced blocks with a plain block between them. In the second row, draw two plain blocks with a pieced block between them. In the third row, repeat the first row.

Example

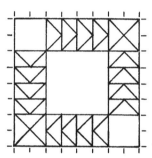

— *Wild Goose Chase block*

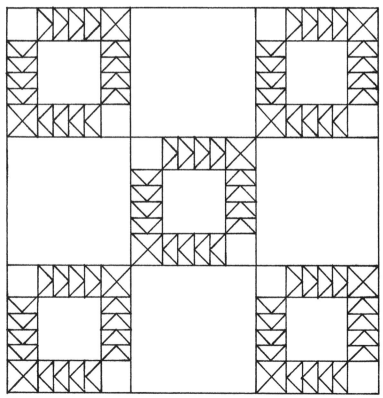

Wild Goose Chase set with alternating plain blocks

Exercises

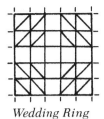

Wedding Ring

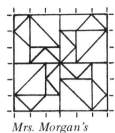

Blocks and Stars

Mrs. Morgan's Choice

C. Sashed Blocks. Draw each of the following unit blocks in a sashed set. Draw three rows of three blocks, with sashing strips between blocks in a row and between rows of blocks. Sashing should be one or two graph squares wide in your drawing.

Example

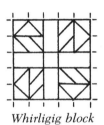

Whirligig block

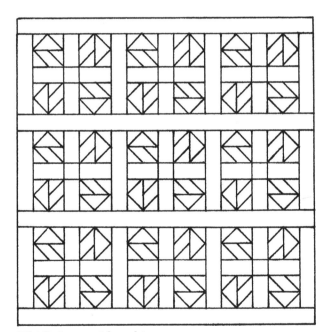

Whirligig set with sashing

Exercises

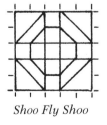

Shoo Fly Shoo

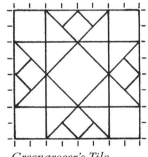

Swing in the Center

Greengrocer's Tile

D. Free Play. Repeat Exercise A, B, or C with the unit block of your choice.

FOUR

Set Variations

The preceding chapter introduced you to three basic sets for arranging unit blocks. The three sets in combination with your choice of unit blocks should provide sufficient design possibilities to keep you entertained indefinitely. But the most rewarding and creative part of designing a quilt comes when you take one step further and explore the methods for changing the set.

Recall the four properties of the unit block:

1. Coloring   3. Proportions
2. Pattern   4. Orientation

These properties also apply to sets. By changing these variables in the set, you can create countless original quilt designs.

Coloring in the Set 7

Just by the way that you color the blocks in the set, you can make them appear to float, create the illusion of a border, simulate a medallion, or establish a very traditional or an unmistakably contemporary look for your quilt.

Making the Blocks Appear to Float. Color can be used to highlight the set structure, or it can be used to obscure it. Sashing strips or alternating plain blocks in colors that contrast with the unit blocks tend to accentuate the checkerboard or sashed effect, isolating the blocks and organizing them into well-defined rows. On the other hand, sashing strips or alternating plain blocks that match the background fabric around the edges of the blocks blend with the neighboring blocks, making the set less obvious. The unit blocks appear to float on the quilt surface. The following examples show blocks set with matching and contrasting plain blocks and sashing strips.

Campfire set with matching plain blocks

Campfire set with contrasting plain blocks

Aunt Sukey's Choice (variation) set with matching sashing

Aunt Sukey's Choice (variation) set with contrasting sashing

Coloring Blocks Differently in the Set. You can color all the blocks identically in the quilt for a traditional look. If you want your quilt to be more contemporary, consider changing the coloring from one row of blocks to the next. By doing this, you can create a quilt with bold stripes of color or gradual, subtle color shifts. You can arrange blocks of similar and dissimilar coloring randomly, concentrically for a medallion effect, or even alternately in checkerboard fashion. The Greenpeace quilt in Plate 8 shows a change in block coloring around the edges of the quilt to create a bordered effect.

Robbing Peter to Pay Paul Sets. A special kind of color change is found in traditional patterns that go by the name of Robbing Peter to Pay Paul. Here, neighboring blocks are colored as opposites. Usually done in just two colors, one block looks like it was made from the shapes cut away from its neighbor. The first figure on page 50 shows a group of blocks colored as opposites. You could use this setting idea for many blocks besides the ones named Robbing Peter to Pay Paul. You might find it interesting to color blocks as opposites in the main shapes of the figure and background and then introduce additional colors as accents, as shown in the second figure.

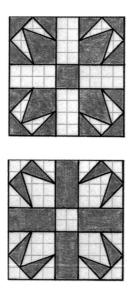

Crosses and Star in a Robbing Peter to Pay Paul set

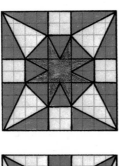

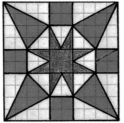

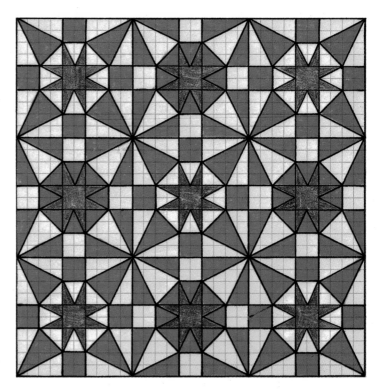

Sparkler in a Robbing Peter to Pay Paul set with an accent color added

Ignoring Unit Block Boundaries. A very dramatic way of changing the design results when the quilt pattern is viewed as a whole, with no regard for unit block boundaries in the coloring. In order to design a quilt like this, you must draw the entire quilt in bare outline form; you then color the patches as a central medallion or however you desire, paying no attention to the division into individual unit blocks. You will have to carefully plan the quilt and pay close attention to your quilt drawing as you construct the quilt because the construction will still be in unit blocks, and these may be of many different colorings. The following illustration shows a quilt colored without regard for unit block divisions.

Compressed Pinwheel colored ignoring unit block boundaries

EXERCISE

CHANGING COLORING IN THE SET

A. Floating Blocks. Color the set pieces (sashes/plain blocks) to match the background of the unit blocks in one set and to contrast in the second set of each pair.

Example

 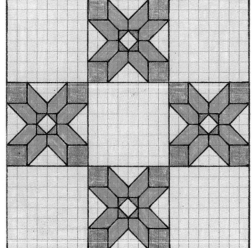

Marigolds set with contrasting plain blocks   *Marigolds set with matching plain blocks*

Exercises

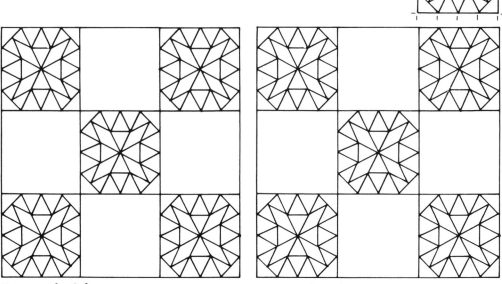

Icing on the Cake   *Icing on the Cake*

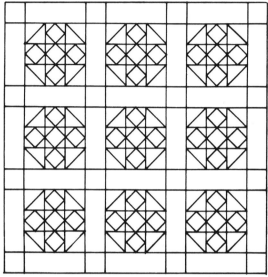

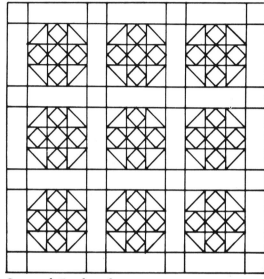

Sawtooth Patchwork   *Sawtooth Patchwork*

B. Robbing Peter to Pay Paul. Color the following set so that the neighboring blocks are opposites. (Suggestion: Introduce accent colors, if desired.)

Example

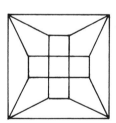

King David's Crown block

King David's Crown in a Robbing Peter to Pay Paul arrangement

Exercise

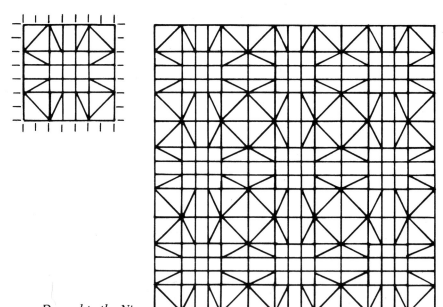

Dressed to the Nines

C. Coloring Blocks Differently. Color the various blocks differently in the set given. (Suggestion: Color the blocks in checkerboard fashion, or color them in rows or rings of matching blocks.)

Example

Radish Roses block

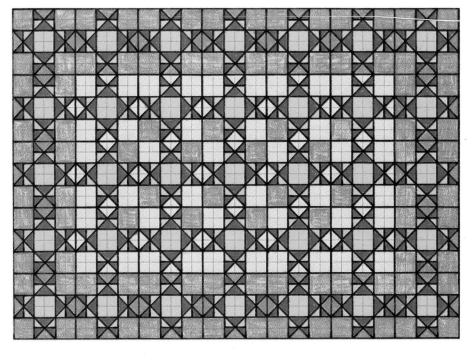

Radish Roses with blocks colored differently

Exercise

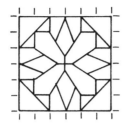

Morning Glory

Exercise   D. Ignoring Block Boundaries. Color the design below without regard to unit block boundaries.

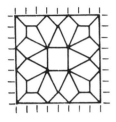

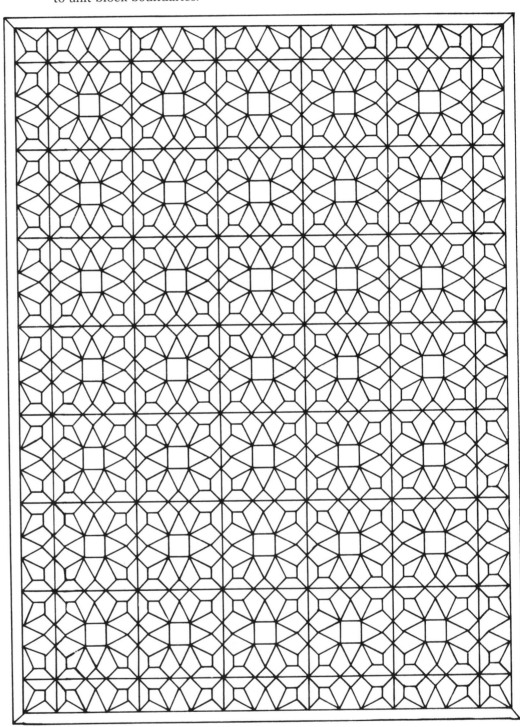

Nirvana

E. Free Play. Draw the block and set of your choice, and color as described in Exercise A, B, C, or D.

Pattern in the Set

The creative part of designing a quilt doesn't have to stop with the selection of a unit block and one of the three basic sets. There are plenty of pattern variations that you might want to explore to make your quilt design distinctive. Consider adding detail to the alternating plain blocks or to the sashing strips between blocks. Embellishing the plain blocks or strips with piecing that echoes some part of the unit block has the effect of drawing the blocks and the set together in an all-over pattern that is more interesting and complete than the isolated blocks would be.

Pieced Sashing. Sashing strips can be changed by simply inserting squares where the horizontal and vertical strips cross. This is especially effective when the squares echo a similar square in the unit block, creating some interplay between block and set. The parasols block is shown with this kind of sashing of squares and strips.

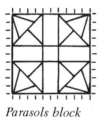

Parasols block

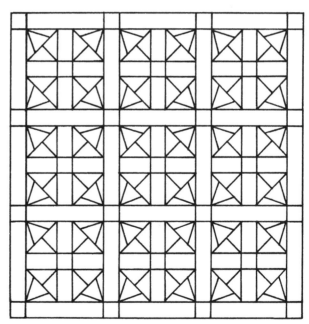

Parasols set with sashing of squares and strips

Another way to change the pattern of the set is to use several sashing strips between blocks, instead of just a single strip. In Lincoln Logs, each block is framed with a band of sashing on four sides; the framed unit is then set in a network of standard sashing strips. Notice how the multiple sashing arrangement repeats the bands in the corners of the unit blocks.

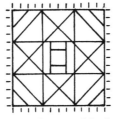

Lincoln Logs block

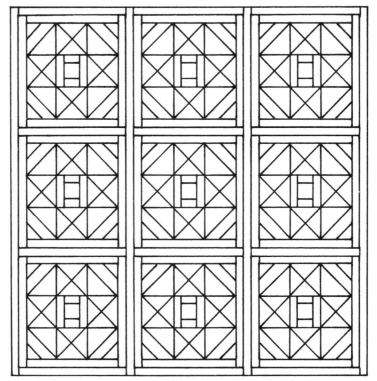

Lincoln Logs set with multiple sashing strips

The sashing strips themselves or the setting squares where the sashes cross can also be pieced in more intricate patterns. The setting squares can be thought of as miniature blocks; any block can be substituted for the plain squares. Of course, since the square is usually small, you should select a block pattern that is fairly simple. Often, you can draw out part of the unit block design and use it for the setting square. The Path and Stiles quilt shows a design with a pieced setting square that repeats a part of the unit block.

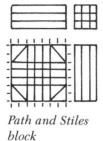

*Path and Stiles
block*

*Path and Stiles set with pieced setting squares
and sashing strips*

Sashing strips can be pieced from rows of triangles, diamonds, squares, or other shapes. Since pieced sashing can be very busy-looking, sometimes it is a good idea to insert plain sashing strips between the pieced sashing and the unit blocks. Pieced sashing is most effective when the piecing relates to shapes in the unit blocks. Green Mountain Star is an example of a quilt set with pieced sashing.

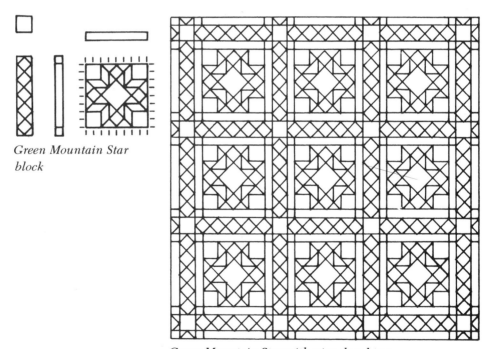

*Green Mountain Star
block*

Green Mountain Star with pieced sashing

Accessory Blocks   *Accessory Blocks.* The blocks that alternate with the unit blocks in checkerboard fashion across the quilt need not be plain. By substituting a simple pieced block for the plain alternating block, you can derive some very interesting and attractive variations. The following illustrations show some simple blocks that work well when alternated with other blocks. I call these simple blocks "accessory blocks."

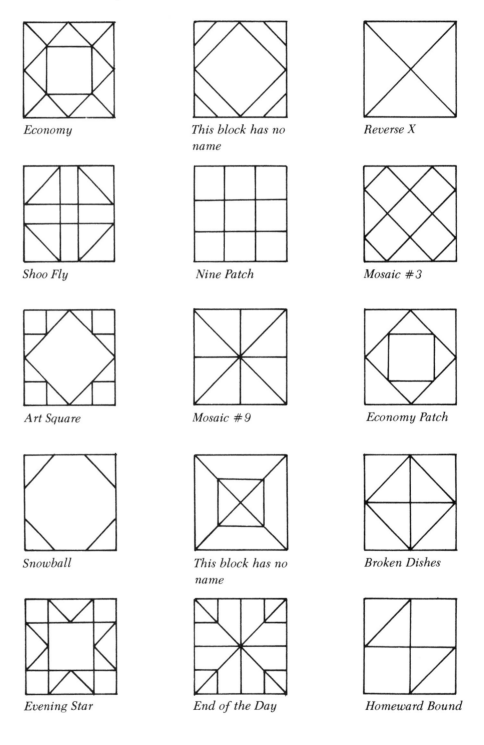

Economy

This block has no name

Reverse X

Shoo Fly

Nine Patch

Mosaic #3

Art Square

Mosaic #9

Economy Patch

Snowball

This block has no name

Broken Dishes

Evening Star

End of the Day

Homeward Bound

Choose an accessory block with lines that complement your block. Then draw the accessory block on a graph grid of the same number of squares as your block. By using an accessory block that is related to the unit block by a similar division of space, you can create an overall pattern that has depth and movement. The individual blocks melt together to form a new design. Here is an example where unit blocks are set with related accessory blocks.

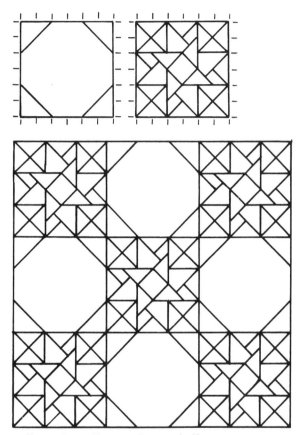

Belle of the Ball set with Snowballs

Combining Different Unit Blocks. This is a natural extension of the idea of using pieced accessory blocks in place of alternating plain blocks in the quilt setting. Two different unit blocks, either traditional or original, can be alternated across the quilt surface. Or you can use more than two different blocks—or even make every block different, as in a sampler quilt. The different blocks can be arranged in several ways in addition to the standard checkerboard arrangement. For example, blocks can be arranged with sashing between them, or they can be arranged in concentric rings, with each ring made from blocks of a different type. The different blocks can radiate from the center or be arranged in rows. One interesting possibility for combining different blocks in a set is to make a number of variations of a single block, with the detail ranging from simple to complex, and then to arrange these blocks to show off the gradation of detail. An example of this is shown in the illustration on page 62.

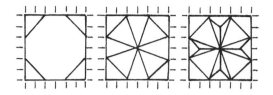

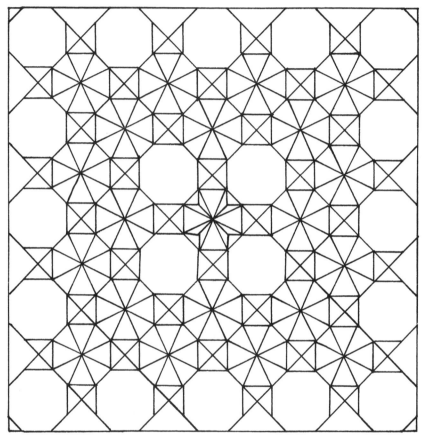

Charlotte's Web

EXERCISE

**PATTERN
VARIATION IN THE
SET**

A. Pieced Sashing. Draw each of the following unit blocks in a set using sashing of squares and strips, multiple strips, or pieced strips/setting squares. Suit the embellishment to the unit blocks. Draw an area of at least three blocks by three blocks. Start by drawing a single unit block. Then in the graph space next to the block, work out the sashing, relating it to the graph squares. On the other side of the sashing, draw another block. Continue drawing unit blocks and sashing strips. In the small squares left over where sashes cross each other, work out your setting square design.

Example

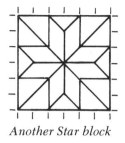

Another Star block

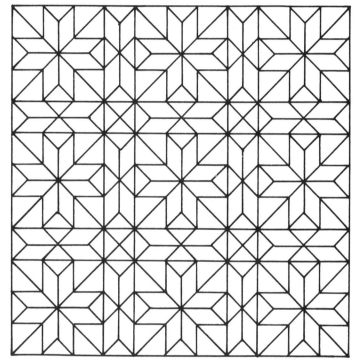

Another Star set with pieced sashing

Exercises

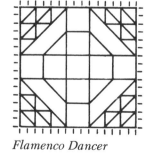

Flamenco Dancer

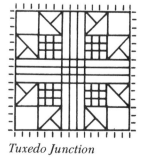

Tuxedo Junction

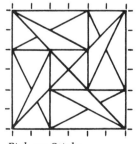

Pick-up Sticks

B. Accessory Blocks. Draw each of the following unit blocks in a set of alternating blocks. Substitute an accessory block from the examples shown on page 60 for the plain block in each design. Choose an accessory block that is divided along lines similar to those in the unit block for more interest.

Example

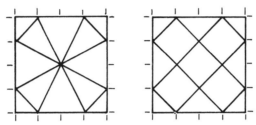

Octagons and Mosaic #3 blocks

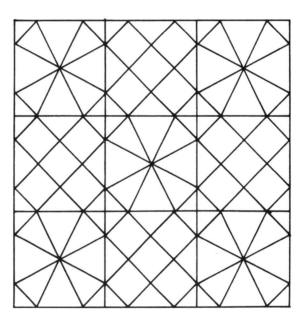

Exercises

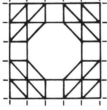

Flying Snowball

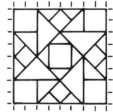

Budding Star

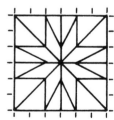

Moonbeams

C. Combining Different Unit Blocks. Draw a quilt design using the block variations given. Arrange them any way that you please.

Exercises

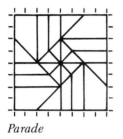

Parade

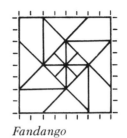

Fandango

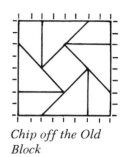

Chip off the Old Block

D. Free Play. Repeat Exercise A, B, or C, using the unit block or blocks of your choice.

Proportions in the Set 9

There are a number of ways that you can modify traditional quilt designs by playing with the proportions of the parts. Some of these changes yield some exciting ideas for contemporary designs. Others produce more traditional-looking results.

Changing the Width of the Sashing. Sashing strips in traditional-style quilts are usually the width of $\frac{1}{8}$ to $\frac{1}{4}$ of the block (or about $1\frac{1}{2}''$ to $3''$ wide). Your unit block might suggest an appropriate width for sashing. If the block is designed around a central panel, you can plan the sashing to match the width of that panel. Or the sash might be made $\frac{1}{4}$ the width of a block covering 4×4 graph squares of $\frac{1}{5}$ the width of a 5×5 block. By relating the width of sashing to some portion of the unit block, you not only tie in the pattern, but you also simplify the task of drawing the sashing on graph paper. Simply follow the graph lines to draw your sashing anywhere from one square wide to about four squares wide. Narrower-than-normal sashing can produce a very interesting effect if it is made in a neutral or unobtrusive color. It almost disappears, allowing the blocks to interact almost as if they were set side by side. The following illustration shows blocks set with narrow sashing.

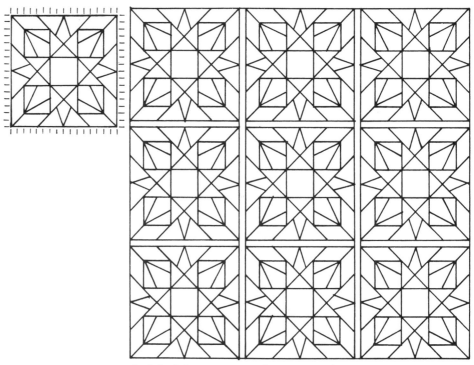

Carlsbad Caverns set with narrow sashing

Wide sashing tends to look heavy, but it might be appropriate in a light color if you want to use the space to show off fine quilting.

Changing the Grid of the Whole Quilt. A very interesting, contemporary design idea is to change size and proportions from block to block in the set. Small and large square blocks, along with rectangular blocks, are arranged in rows of varying widths. Just as you drew a new grid in order to change proportions within the unit block, you can draw a new grid to represent the quilt and the blocks in it. Within the grid, you may have several different sizes and shapes of blocks. Draw the blocks to fit the proportions of each. Here, the first figure shows a quilt grid redrawn this way, and the second figure shows the blocks drawn in this new grid.

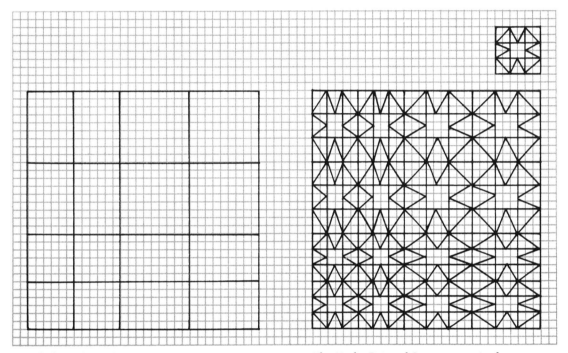

Whole quilt grid

The Eight-Pointed Star on a revised quilt grid

Blocks of Different Sizes. Small and large blocks can be combined in fairly traditional-looking quilts or in very modern ones. You can use small and large blocks of different patterns, the same pattern, or even blocks and quarter-blocks for interesting effects. It is helpful to choose block sizes that are somehow related so that the blocks fit together easily. The illustration on page 68 shows a quilt design of blocks and quarter-blocks.

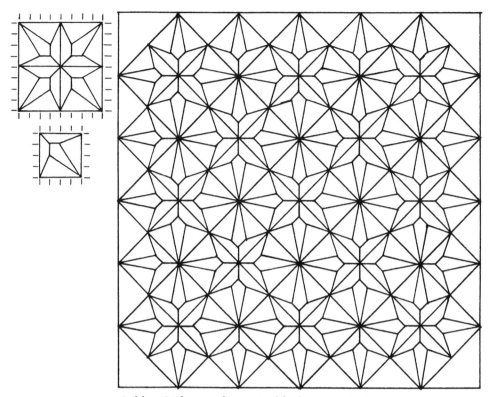

Golden Girl set with quarter blocks around edges

EXERCISE

CHANGING PROPORTIONS IN THE SET

A. Unobtrusive Sashing. Draw the block given in a set with sashing one graph square wide. Color the sashing inconspicuously.

Example

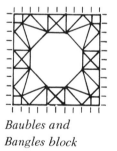

Baubles and Bangles block

Baubles and Bangles set with narrow sashing

Exercise

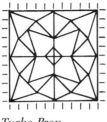

Turbo-Prop

B. Blocks of Different Sizes. Combine the two blocks given in an arrangement of your choice.

Example

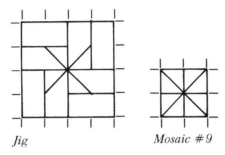

Jig   *Mosaic #9*

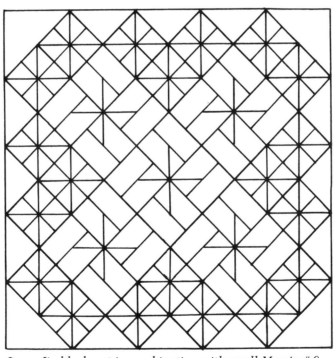

Large Jig blocks set in combination with small Mosaic #9 blocks

Exercise

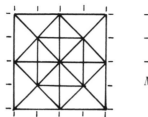

Mosaic #9

Peace and Plenty

C. Changing the Grid of the Whole Quilt. Fill in the grid with the block shown. Change the size or proportions of the block to fit each square of the grid.

Example

Windmill

Windmill set in a revised grid

Exercise

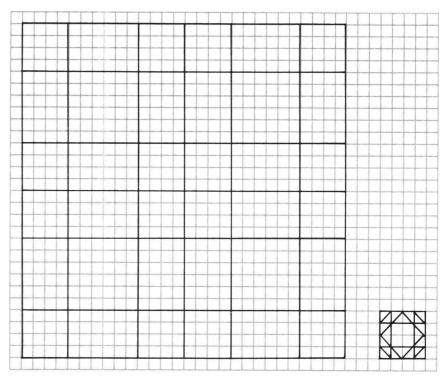

Revised grid   *The Cypress*

D. Free Play. Repeat Exercise A, B, or C with the unit block of your choice.

Orientation in the Set

10

Orientation refers to the way the blocks are positioned—that is, the way they tilt and the way they are lined up relative to each other. The blocks can be set straight in line with the edges of the quilt or on the diagonal; they can also be in even rows or staggered arrangements.

Diagonal Sets. All three of the basic sets can be used to arrange blocks on the diagonal. Diagonal arrangements of adjacent blocks, alternating plain blocks, and sashed blocks are shown in the following examples. Diagonal sets need a band of triangles around the outside of the quilt to square off the edges. The triangles around the perimeter of the quilt can be plain, or they can be pieced if the unit block can be easily divided in half diagonally.

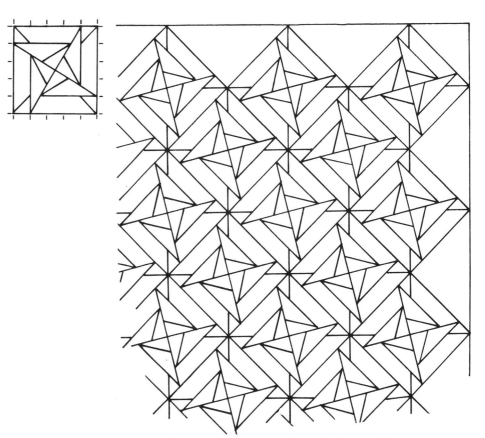

Cloak and Dagger in a diagonal set of adjacent blocks

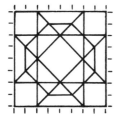

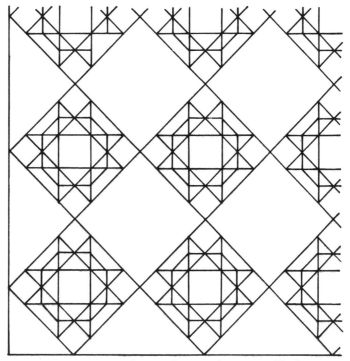

Georgetown Loop in a diagonal set of alternating blocks

Both within the set and within the unit block, those lines running parallel to the edges of the quilt tend to be accentuated. For this reason, a diagonal set softens the boxy effect of sashing and alternating blocks. Furthermore, a diagonal orientation, by setting the unit blocks on end, can give a distinctly different appearance to the block. Some blocks benefit more from a diagonal set; others are shown to best advantage in a straight set. Usually, a block will appear more lively in one orientation than the other. In your choice of orientation, you should take this into consideration. You can preview the effect of changing block orientation by tilting the drawing of the block.

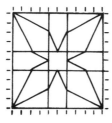

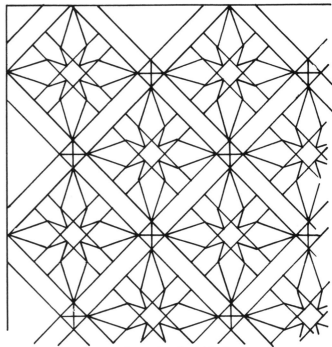

Stardust in a diagonal set of sashed blocks

Staggered Sets. Staggering the blocks provides another possibility for changing the set. A row of blocks can be sandwiched between two rows that are offset by a half-block, as in the next example. You can stagger blocks to achieve effective variations of adjacent, sashed, or alternating block sets. This set variation is most successful with unit blocks that can easily be divided in half horizontally.

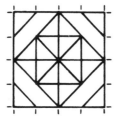

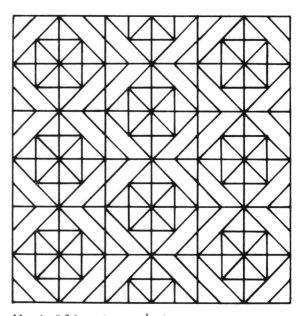

Mosaic #2 in a staggered set

The Picket Fence or Streak o' Lightning Set, shown in the next illustration, combines a diagonal orientation with a staggered arrangement of blocks. In this set, rows of alternating plain *triangles* and unit blocks are constructed, and adjacent rows are staggered by a half-block split diagonally.

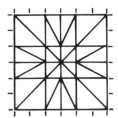

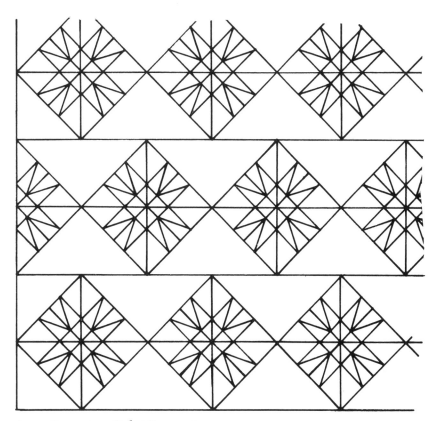

Laser Beams in a Picket Fence set

Tilting Asymmetrical Blocks. Asymmetrical unit blocks can be turned in different directions in the quilt to create an incredible variety of exciting patterns. Asymmetrical blocks, you will recall, are those which are not identical in all four corners. The asymmetry can be the result of coloring, pattern, or proportion. In any case, asymmetrical blocks can all be tipped the same direction, or they can tilt alternately one direction, then another for different effects. The illustrations on page 76 and 77 show a few of the possible arrangements for asymmetrical blocks.

*Compressed
Pinwheel Blocks Set
in a Few of the
Possible
Arrangements*

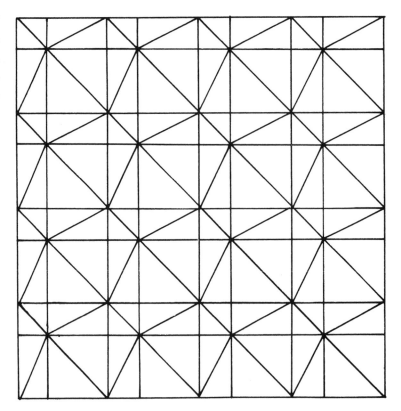

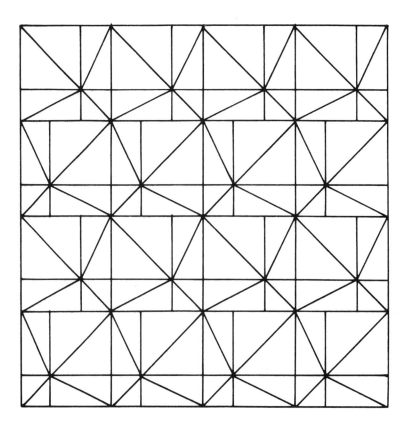

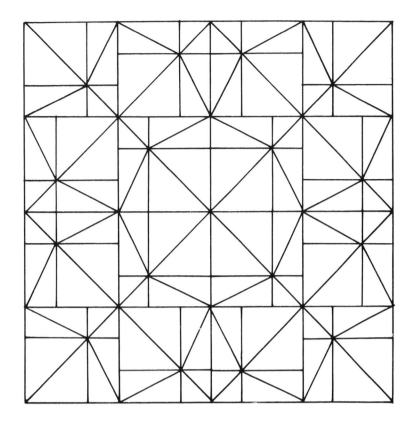

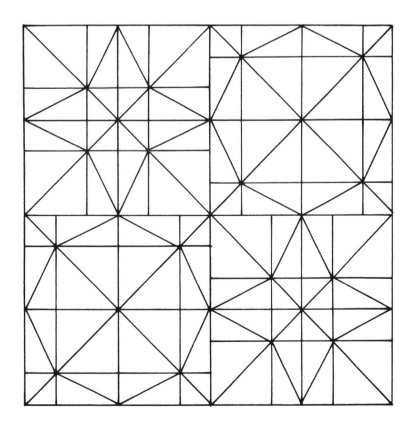

The Barn Raising, Straight Furrows, and Sunshine and Shadows sets illustrated here offer three additional models for varying the orientation of asymmetrical blocks. These sets are traditionally associated with Log Cabin blocks, but they will work effectively to set any asymmetrical block that can be visually split in half along the diagonal. The illustrations on page 80 show a number of asymmetrical unit blocks that are suitable for arrangement in sets of this kind. Many other blocks can be adapted to fit these models simply by coloring them asymmetrically.

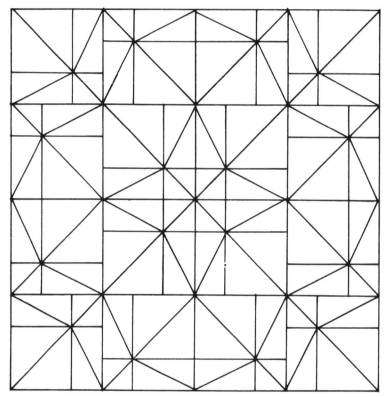

Barn Raising set

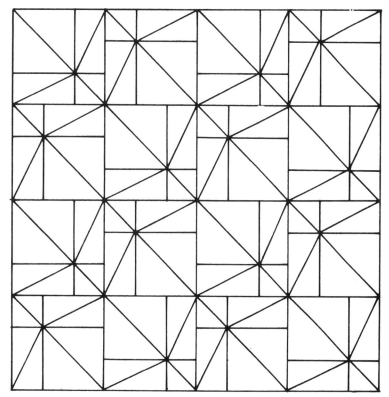

Straight Furrows set

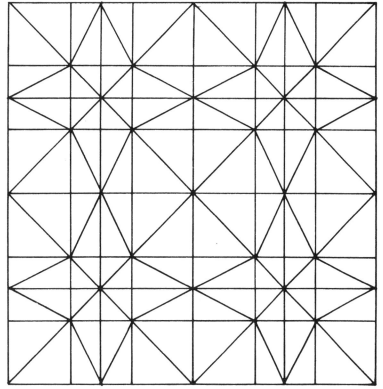

Sunshine and Shadows set

Some Asymmetrical Blocks

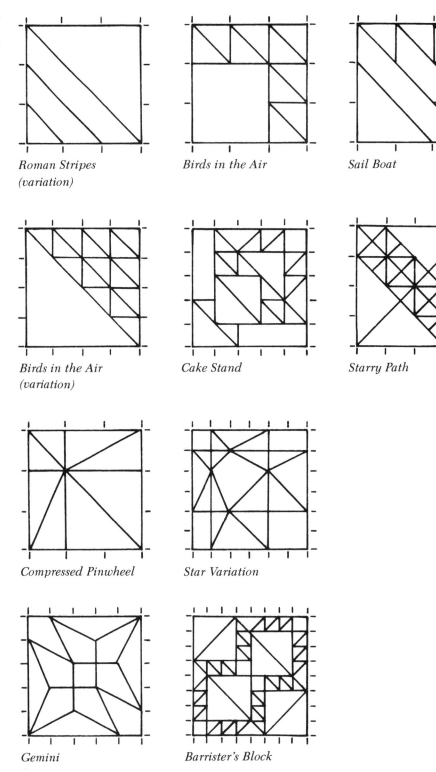

Roman Stripes
(variation)

Birds in the Air

Sail Boat

Birds in the Air
(variation)

Cake Stand

Starry Path

Compressed Pinwheel

Star Variation

Gemini

Barrister's Block

EXERCISE

CHANGING ORIENTATION OF BLOCKS IN THE SET

A. Diagonal Sets. Draw each of the following unit blocks in a diagonal set. (Note: Draw the blocks straight on the graph paper. The edges of the quilt will be on the diagonal of the paper.)

Example

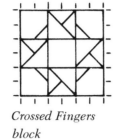

Crossed Fingers block

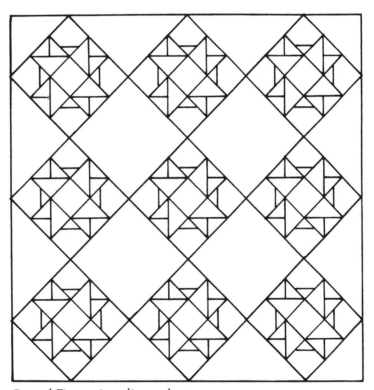

Crossed Fingers in a diagonal set

Exercises

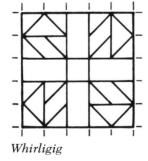

Whirligig

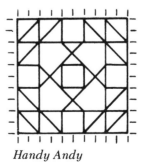

Handy Andy

B. Staggered Sets. Draw each of the following unit blocks in an appropriate staggered set. Offset the blocks in adjacent rows by a half-block. (Suggestion: Try Streak o' Lightning set of diagonal blocks set in rows with alternating plain triangles.)

Example

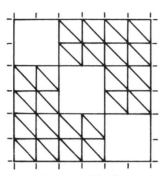

Winged Square block

Winged Square in a staggered set

Exercises

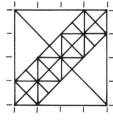

Starry Path

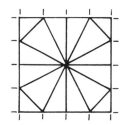

Connecticut

C. Sets of Asymmetrical Blocks. Draw the following asymmetrical unit block in an adjacent block set, varying the tilt of the blocks. (Suggestion: If you like, follow the models for Barn Raising, Straight Furrows, and Sunshine and Shadows sets.)

Example

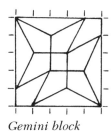

Gemini block

Gemini set in a Barn Raising set

Exercise

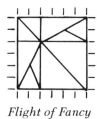

Flight of Fancy

D. Free Play. Repeat Exercise A, B, or C with the block of your choice.

FIVE

Quilts Made Without Unit Blocks

We have seen the wide range of quilt designs possible from arrangements of unit blocks and sets. The popularity and appeal of these designs are easy to understand. Still, there are a couple of other quilt design formats that are worth exploring.

The quilts that we have studied so far are made from rows of blocks across and down the quilt. Strippie quilts are made from rows of blocks (or other units) in one direction only. Medallion quilts are made not from rows, but from concentric rings of blocks or border units surrounding a central design area.

The next two chapters discuss these two different design modes and how to apply your unit block expertise to these new formats to create unique and lovely quilts.

Strippie Quilts 11

Traditionally, a strippie quilt was one made by simply sewing together a few strips of fabric. It was quilted in straight bands of different widths and different designs extending across the quilt. Strippie quilts provided a good vehicle for fancy quilting without all the fancy figuring required to make a quilting motif round a corner gracefully.

I am using the term "strippie quilt" here in a broader sense to mean all quilts of a certain format. These are quilts made in rows in one direction only. The rows need not be made of identifiable unit blocks. Rows can be lengthwise, crosswise, or diagonal. They can be divided by sashing or not. All rows can be the same, they can be different and stand alone, or they can combine to form an all-over pattern.

Rows of Unit Blocks A strippie quilt can be made from unit blocks joined side by side in rows, with the rows separated by sashing. Unlike the usual sashed set, this arrangement has sashing only between rows, not between blocks. This strippie setting allows some of the interplay of adjacent block sets as well as some of the orderliness of sashing. Mosaic #2 shows a strippie quilt made from unit blocks.

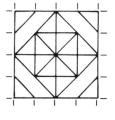

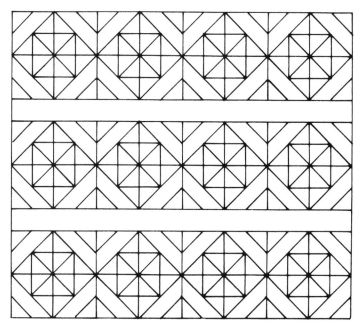

Mosaic #2

Departing from Unit Blocks. Your block and set drawings sometimes result in designs that would be more efficient if made from units other than the unit blocks. Seams might be eliminated between adjacent patches colored to match, for example. When you eliminate these seams, the unit block no longer exists, so the quilt must be made in rows of other units in the strippie format. Here is an example that shows how a quilt is designed this way.

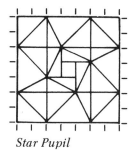

Star Pupil

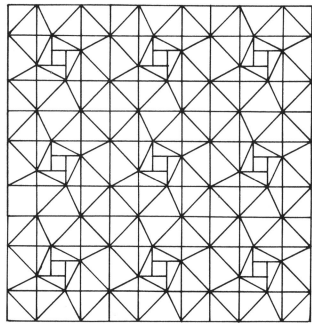

Blocks set side by side

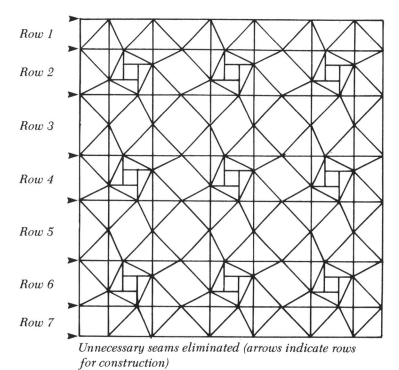

Unnecessary seams eliminated (arrows indicate rows for construction)

Sometimes you can add a shape between unit blocks in your design. The shape bridges the unit blocks and strings them together in a row of nonblock units. The next illustration is an example of this. The strippie idea once again provides the format for joining these units into a quilt.

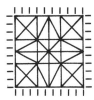

Optical Illusion set with bridging units

In both of these cases, unit blocks provide the inspiration for the quilt designs, but the blocks are abandoned as the designs are refined. In the end, the quilts are not made from blocks at all, but they are made in rows, strippie style.

Strippie quilts don't have to be designed from unit blocks. If you are familiar with Seminole piecing, I am sure that you can visualize strippie quilts designed from Seminole elements. (The Further Reading section includes a good reference on Seminole piecing.) Pieced border designs also provide some good ideas for strippie quilt designs. The Angel's Flight quilt in Plate 4 was designed from a pieced border motif.

EXERCISE

STRIPPIE QUILTS

A. Rows of Unit Blocks. Draw each of the following blocks in a set with blocks set side by side in a row and with sashing between the rows. (Suggestion: Try using a diagonal set for one of the blocks.)

Example

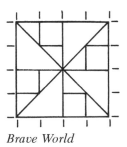

Brave World

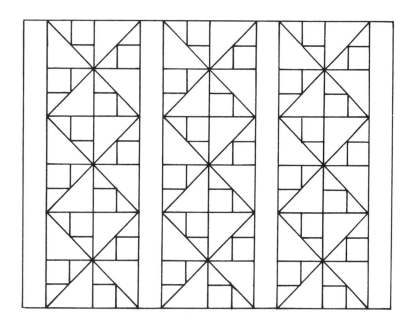

Exercises

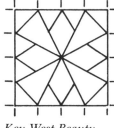

Key West Beauty

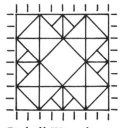

Pinball Wizard

B. Eliminating Seams. Draw the following unit block in a setting of adjacent blocks, all colored the same. Study the arrangement to see where seams between blocks might be eliminated for a more effective design. Redraw the pattern with unnecessary seams deleted (or simply erase those seam lines from your original drawing). Plan how you would construct the quilt from nonblock rows.

Example

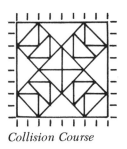

Collision Course

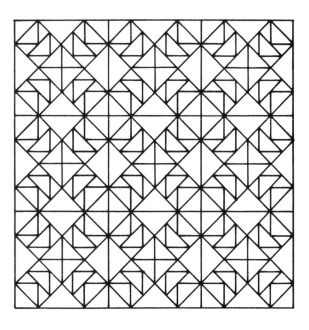

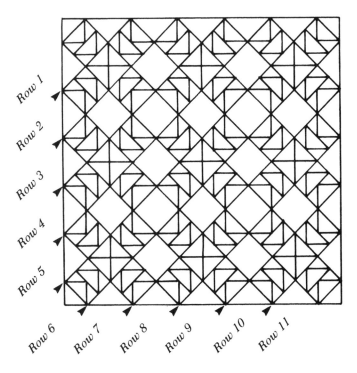

Exercise

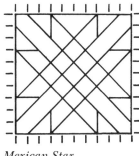

Mexican Star

C. Bridging Blocks. Draw the following unit block in a set with other patches bridging the space between blocks. Study the arrangement to see how you would construct the quilt from rows (or strips) of blocks and other units.

Example

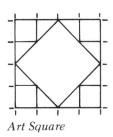

Art Square

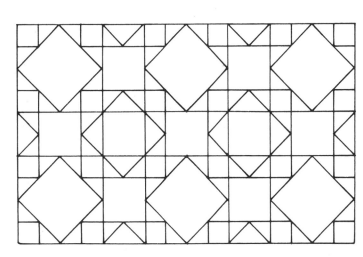

Exercise

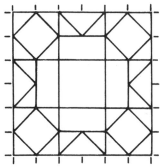

Rolling Squares

D. Free Play. Starting with a unit block of your choice, design a strippie quilt as described in Exercise A, B, or C.

Medallion Quilts 12

Medallion quilts are made from a central design area surrounded by several borders. Rather than being made from rows, medallion quilts are made concentrically, starting in the center and building outward. These quilts are also designed starting with the center.

The Medallion Center. The central design area, or central medallion, is usually made from a single unit block or a small grouping of blocks. Since the central medallion will be the focus of the quilt, the block or blocks should be fairly elaborate—worthy of the many borders. An ordinary block can be adapted for a central medallion easily. For example, four asymmetrical blocks, all pointing outward, as shown in Fig. 1 below, make a suitable medallion center. Or a single block can be embellished, with shapes added around it, as in Figs. 2–3, for a central medallion.

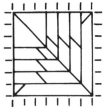

1 Modern Flame

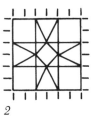

2

3 Mum's the Word

Borders. The borders can be made in pieced strips, triangular units, or a combination of the two. The following illustrations show a few of the different formats possible for medallion quilts. Bands of blocks, blocks with seams eliminated between them, or blocks with other shapes bridging them, as discussed in Chapter 11, can be used in the border strips. As well, repeating shapes such as triangles, diamonds, or squares make attractive border strips. To fill the triangular units, blocks and smaller blocks or partial blocks can be used.

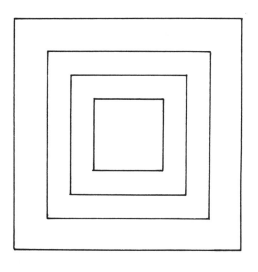

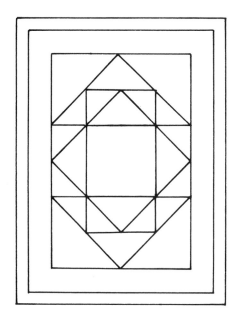

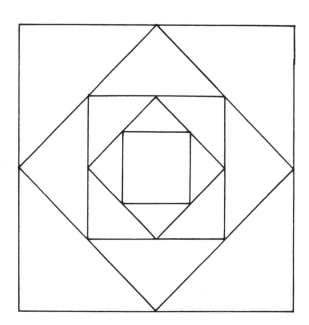

Borders must be carefully planned in order for the corners to match and the design to look natural and complete. By choosing border designs related to the center, perhaps with a repeat equal to half the size of the center block, you can make it easier to design a medallion quilt with fluid borders. The next illustration shows a medallion quilt with borders related to the medallion center.

Another way of assuring the perfect fit of borders is to insert plain strips between the pieced borders or between the border and the central medallion. Any two pieced units can be made to fit each other with the insertion of a plain strip of just the right width between them. The example on page 95 shows a medallion quilt designed with plain strips between the pieced parts.

It is easier to design a square medallion quilt than a rectangular one. For a square quilt, you only have to work out the corner treatment once, then repeat it for the other three corners. For a rectangular quilt, you will have to juggle border strips of two lengths, and work out a corner treatment that will work for both of them.

Once you are comfortable playing with graph paper, you should be able to design medallion quilts with the same ease that you design quilts made from rows.

EXERCISE

MEDALLION QUILTS

A. The Medallion Center. Add shapes around the blocks given to create a suitable central medallion.

Example

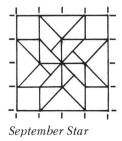

September Star

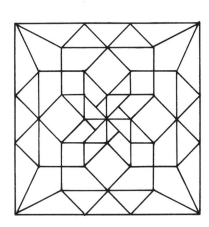

Exercises

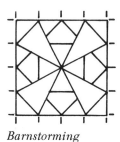

Barnstorming

Star Puzzle

B. Four-Block Medallion Center. Arrange these asymmetrical blocks in groups of four to design medallion centers.

Example

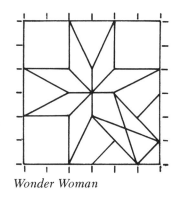

Wonder Woman

Exercises

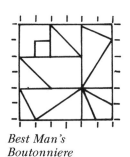

*Best Man's
Boutonniere*

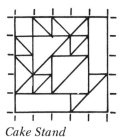

Cake Stand

C. The Medallion Quilt. On graph paper draw a medallion quilt using the center block and border repeat given. Start the design in the center. Add other borders of your own design, if desired.

Exercise

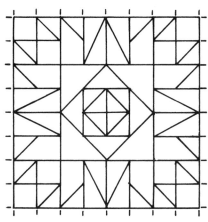

Miss B's Roses, center block

Border unit

D. Free Play. Design a medallion quilt, starting with the block of your choice for the central medallion, and adding borders to suit it.

SIX

Borders

Up to this point, you have been playing with small segments of quilts—unit blocks or a few blocks arranged in a set. As you settle on a design to make and begin preparing a quilt plan, you should take time to think about border designs. Every quilt design can be enhanced by an appropriate border. If you work out a border design now, before you have figured the specifications for your quilt, you can easily incorporate the borders into your quilt plan. This way, your borders won't look like an afterthought; they will be the perfect finishing touch for a coherent design.

Designing Fitting Borders 13

Quilts and borders are a natural combination. Most often, quilts are used on beds, and the planes of the bed define distinct visual areas: a more-or-less square top surface and a long, narrow drop. A change of pattern and color around the edges of the quilt—a border—is perfectly suited to this visual format. Wall quilts, too, call for borders to complete them. Just as a frame completes a painting and keeps it from fading into the wall behind it, a border completes and defines a wall quilt.

An effective border treatment can make the difference between an ordinary quilt and a masterpiece. A border should be a natural extension of the central motif, continuing lines, highlighting colors, or recombining shapes introduced in the main body of the quilt. In order for the border to effectively define the quilt, though, it must also offer some contrast. A change of color concentration or a simplification of pattern in the border will provide the flourish needed to complete the quilt.

Border Width. How much border is the right amount for your quilt? I can't tell you one perfect answer. The same quilt might be finished equally attractively with a number of different border widths. The success depends on the nature of the quilt pattern and the completeness of the border design. If your quilt pattern takes a lot of space to develop, an extra row or two of blocks and a narrow border strip might serve the quilt better than a wide border. On the other hand, if your quilt is large and contains many repetitive blocks, a wide border will provide a welcome change. Sometimes constraints of block and quilt size will dictate a border of certain dimensions. The width of the border is really not so important as the suitability of the border pattern to the rest of the quilt. Keep in mind that the border should set off the quilt to advantage without upstaging the main design.

Color in the Border. Whatever color you choose for your border, consider that it will have the effect of highlighting that color or fabric in the rest of the design. It may change the perceived color distribution strongly. If you want to play up or accent a fabric, by all means use it in the border. Do not introduce an all-new color scheme in the border. One or two new fabrics in colors already established in the center of the quilt might be used successfully. Or a new color that you have selected to match a minor color in one of the prints might be justified. Generally, though, it is advisable to stick to the palette of colors and specific fabrics used in the quilt center and simply rearrange them in new proportions. For example, if your quilt is predominantly light, cut down on the light-colored fabrics in the border.

Planning Pieced Borders. A pieced border can enhance the quilt with its continuity, but if it is ill planned, it can detract from the overall design. Ideally, the pieced border should frame the quilt in an unbroken chain that rounds the corners fluidly. This sounds difficult, but it doesn't have to be. Here are a few ways to accomplish perfectly fitting pieced borders without an engineering feat.

The easiest way to design a pieced border to fit the quilt is to make the border from modified unit blocks. By simply altering the existing block for the outer ring of the quilt—either by changing the color emphasis or adding or eliminating pattern detail—a handsome frame for the quilt can be easily achieved. If the blocks in the quilt are set with sashing, simply extend the sashing into the borders. Greenpeace, in Plate 8, shows an example of a quilt designed this way.

Another easy way to design a border to fit is to draw four blocks representing the corner of the quilt. Notice the way the blocks interact to form new shapes where they join. Draw patches in the border space to complete these shapes on the outer edges of the blocks. Fill in the remaining space in the border with other shapes as you see fit. Work out a corner block related to the border. The next two illustrations show how to design borders using this method. The quilts in Plates 1 and 3 have borders of this type.

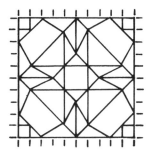

Shangri-la block

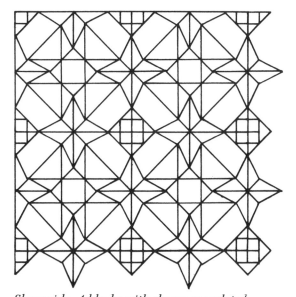

Shangri-la, 4 blocks with shapes completed around edges

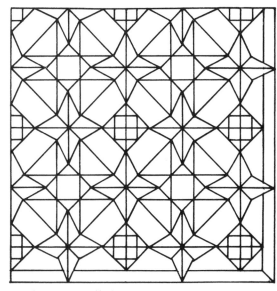

Border spaces filled in

A pleasing, naturally fitting border can be devised by drawing four corner blocks and simply extending straight or angled lines from each point or seam along the block edges. The following example shows a quilt border designed this way. The many borders in the X-O-X-O-X quilt in Plate 5 were also designed using this method.

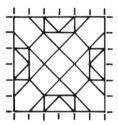

Swing in the Center

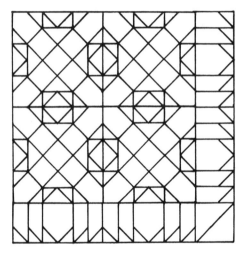

Simple bands of triangles, diamonds, squares, or other shapes can form lovely borders. A few examples follow.

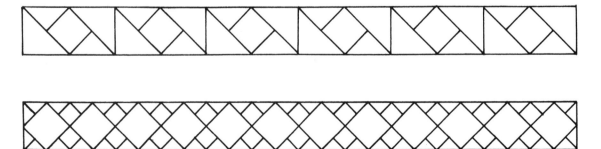

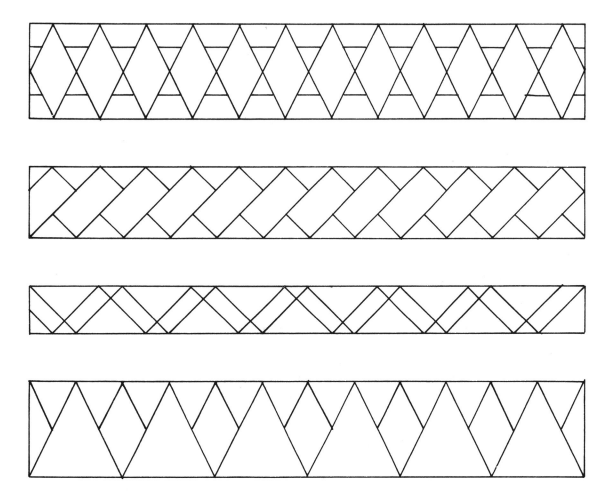

Choose a band that echoes shapes in your quilt block, or design an original band using shapes from your block. Draw a few repeats, and work out on paper how to round the corner. If necessary, reverse the design at the center of each side of the quilt in order to have symmetry in the four corners of the border. Here's an example that shows a border reversed at the center of each side, with corners worked out.

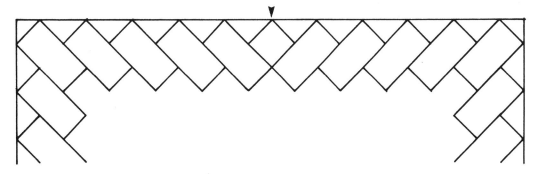

Borders reversed at center (marked with arrow) and corners worked out

Borders of this kind will *look* natural with your quilt blocks, but the fit may not be so natural. To achieve fluid borders and graceful corners, you may have to insert a plain strip between the border and the center of the quilt. (This will probably look best anyway, because the points of the border and blocks won't necessarily line up in designs of this type.) Any pieced border can be made to fit any quilt design by inserting a plain strip between the two. The plain strip permits you to work out an attractive corner solution without being concerned about fitting the dimensions of the quilt center. You simply plan your pieced border slightly longer than necessary to fit the center of the quilt. Then you can either draw the quilt and borders to scale (see Chapters 14–16), or you can just construct the quilt and borders, measure them, compare the lengths, and divide the difference by two to find the width of the plain strip required. (Don't forget to add seam allowances to the width of the plain strip when you cut it out.) For a rectangular quilt, you will need to figure the plain strip widths separately for the sides and top and bottom of the quilt. Plate 7 shows Barrister's Block, a quilt made with a border band designed in this way.

EXERCISE

DESIGNING BORDERS

A. Modified Unit Blocks. Four blocks representing the corner of a quilt are shown along with five block outlines for border blocks. Fill in the details of the border blocks, making them modified versions of the unit blocks.

Exercise

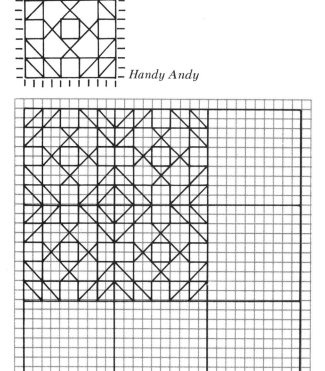

Handy Andy

B. Completing Shapes on the Edge. Draw four of the blocks given. Complete important shapes along the outside edges of the blocks, and then fill in around these shapes to complete borders.

Example

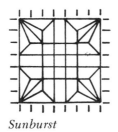

Sunburst

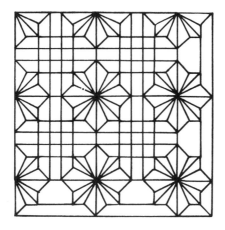

Exercise

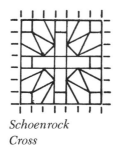

Schoenrock Cross

C. Line Extensions. Draw the given block, four times, then draw borders around two sides. Simply extend lines from each point or seam at the block edges.

Example

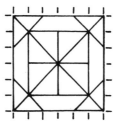

The Range's Pride

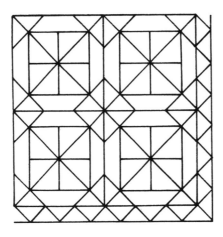

Exercise

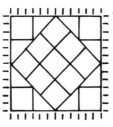

Union Square

D. Pieced Bands. Design a simple band of repeating shapes suitable for the block shown. Work out a design for the border corners.

Example

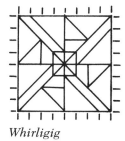

Whirligig

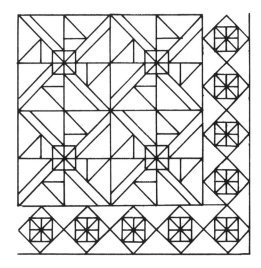

Exercise

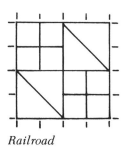

Railroad

E. Free Play. Design a border for the block and set of your choice. Use the method described in Exercise A, B, C, or D.

SEVEN

Quilt Plans

After some experimentation with unit blocks and sets and their variations, you may arrive at a pattern that you would like to use in a quilt. The next few lessons deal with the subject of translating your pattern sketch into a quilt design of appropriate dimensions.

Desired Quilt Size

You may have drawn your colored pattern sketch with a definite purpose in mind for the quilt. If not, now is the time to think about whether you plan to use the quilt as a decorative piece on the wall, a lap throw, or a bedcovering. Your sketch may dictate certain size requirements or color schemes that provide clues about how you can best use the quilt. For example, the pattern may have many, many pieces and need considerable space for the design to develop. In this case, you might want to make a fairly large bed quilt. Or your drawing may duplicate the color scheme in your dining room, suggesting the idea of a small wall quilt to hang by the table.

Wall quilts can be as small as 10 inches or as large as 10 feet. If you are planning a wall quilt, decide just where you want to hang it so you can design the quilt to fit the space.

Lap throws are usually about 4 feet wide and 5 to 6 feet long. You can make a throw to barely cover your legs, or you can make one big enough to snuggle under right up to your ears. Duplicate the size of a favorite old afghan, or experiment with a folded sheet to decide on a comfortable size for you.

Bed quilts can be made in a wide range of sizes. You probably have in mind a particular bed on which to display your quilt. Standard bed dimensions (length and width of the mattress) are listed below.

STANDARD BED DIMENSIONS	
Crib	27″ × 52″
Youth	33″ × 66″
Twin	39″ × 75″
Full	54″ × 75″
Queen	60″ × 80″
King	76″ × 80″

To determine the correct quilt size for your bed, you will want to consider not only bed dimensions, but also drop. The drop is the distance beyond the top surface of the bed that the quilt falls at the sides and foot of the bed. A bedspread falls to the floor, having a drop of 20 to 21 inches. (Measure the distance from the top surface of the bed to the floor for the exact dimension.) A coverlet typically has a drop of 9 to 15 inches. It is used with a dust ruffle and should be long enough to cover the mattress without necessarily covering the box springs. A comforter is made only slightly larger than the mattress dimensions. It is designed to cover the occupant of the bed.

Next, you will need to decide how to treat the pillows. A commercial bedspread allows as much as 12 inches extra in length to cover the pillows. On a thick quilt, this can be rather bulky, and it adds considerably to the time and work involved in making the quilt. You may prefer to add only a few inches to the length and gently slope the quilt over the pillows. As an alternative, you can make matching pillow shams or pillow cases and forget about a pillow allowance on the quilt.

By now, you should have a fairly clear concept of the way you want your quilt to fit the bed. However, you may be disappointed in your results unless you take into account one more factor. Your quilt will contract a couple of inches after stuffing and quilting or tying. You should add 2 to 4 inches to both length and width to allow for the anticipated contraction. (Two inches will suffice for small quilts or thin quilts; add more for larger or thicker ones.)

To figure out your desired quilt size, consider length and width separately. First calculate width. Simply add the drop for one side, then the other, to the width of the mattress. Then add 2 to 4 inches for contraction. To calculate quilt length: Add the drop at the bottom to the mattress length; next, add allowance for pillow tuck, if any; finally, add 2 to 4 inches for contraction.

Example. Suppose that you want to make a quilt to use as a coverlet on a double bed. You've decided on a 9″ drop and a 2″ pillow tuck. To figure the quilt width, you take the 54″ mattress width and add 9″ + 9″ for drop on two sides. This gives you 72″. Now add 2″ for contraction, for a total of 74″. To figure quilt length, add the 75″ mattress length + 9″ drop + 2″ pillow tuck + 2″ for contraction, for a total of 88″. Your desired quilt size, then, is 74″ × 88″.

The following chart will give you some idea of the usual range of dimensions for commercial bedding. Use it for guidance and comparison.

COMMERCIAL BEDDING SIZES

	COMFORTER	BEDSPREAD
Twin	68″ × 86″	80″ × 106″
Full	76″ × 86″	96″ × 106″
Queen	92″ × 86″	101″ × 118″
King	104″ × 86″	118″ × 118″

EXERCISE

FIGURING THE DESIRED QUILT SIZE

Free Play. Use the following formula to determine the desired size for your quilt.

		WIDTH	LENGTH
1. Dimensions of bed:		inches	inches
2. Add for drop	left side:	+ inches	XXXXXXXXXXX
	right side:	+ inches	XXXXXXXXXXX
	bottom:	XXXXXXXXXXX	+ inches
3. Add for pillow tuck:		XXXXXXXXXXX	+ inches
4. Add for contraction:		+ inches	+ inches
Equals TOTAL:		inches	by inches

Choosing a Scale for Your Pattern

15

Once you have decided on a pattern and calculated the desired dimensions for your quilt, you must decide on a scale. Your pattern sketch is a representation in miniature of your quilt. You must decide how much to enlarge the pattern when you translate your drawing into actual quilt patches. How big will the smallest patch be? (Or how big will the block be?) One graph square in your drawing will represent how many inches in your quilt? Your decision should be influenced by both esthetic and practical considerations.

When you decide on a scale for your pattern, you are setting the size for your unit block. The size of the block influences the character of the quilt as a whole. Small blocks usually give a quaint, traditional appearance to the quilt, while large ones yield a more expansive, uncluttered, modern look. Furthermore, your scale will determine the number of times the block pattern must be repeated in order to cover your size quilt. A bed quilt composed of a single, simple unit block might lack charm. Repetition is an important part of the appeal of most quilt patterns. Clearly, your scale must be small enough to allow your block design to be repeated a reasonable number of times across the quilt surface. However, the smaller the scale, the more unit blocks will be required to cover a given area and, therefore, the more work will be involved in the project.

You should balance the two factors when you decide on the scale so that your project will be both practical to make and pleasing to view.

As a general rule, a comfortable project for a beginner should have no more than about 400–600 pieces. This could take the form of a baby quilt or wall quilt of small pieces, or a full-sized bed quilt of relatively large pieces. (Tiny pieces are a bit trickier to handle; large pieces take more time to cut and sew.)

Sometimes the scale will be dictated by outside factors. Perhaps you are planning to center a small floral print in one square patch. You may have to make that patch a specific size to fit the printed motif. Choose your scale on the basis of that patch. Similarly, you may want to use a particular quilting template in a patch. In that case, you will want to choose your scale accordingly.

Example. Let's go back to the example introduced in the last chapter and continue working out our quilt plan. Suppose you have decided to make your quilt in the Star Gazing pattern sketched on page 113. Your designed quilt size, as we figured on page 111, is 74″ × 88″. You are an advanced-beginner quilter with a fair measure of patience and good basic sewing skills. You like updated traditional-style quilts with lots of repetition and fairly small pieces, and you don't mind investing some time on the project. You decide that 1½″ is a good size for the smallest triangle in the block. Since the smallest triangle is one graph square high in your drawing, your scale is 1 square = $1\frac{1}{2}''$. At this scale, one block will measure 12″ (8 graph squares $\times$ $1\frac{1}{2}''$ per square equals 12″). Roughly 6 $\times$ 7 blocks will fit your desired quilt size for a total of 1,722 pieces, which seems to be in line with your intentions. Make a note of your scale (in this example, 1 square = $1\frac{1}{2}''$) for use in drawing your quilt plan later.

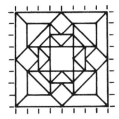

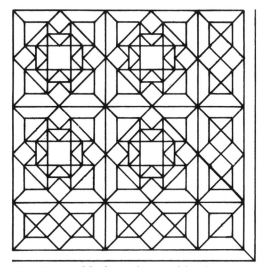

Star Gazing blocks with pieced border

EXERCISE

CHOOSING A SCALE FOR YOUR PATTERN

Free Play. Ask yourself the following questions to help you choose a scale for your design.

1. How much repetition do you feel is necessary or appropriate for the success of your design?
2. Do you prefer to work with small patches or large ones?
3. Are you impatient, unsure of your skills or interest, or in a hurry? (If so, you'd better plan on relatively few pieces.)
4. Are you aiming to win a prize or challenge yourself with intricate work? (If so, make your scale small.)
5. Keeping in mind your answers to the questions above (and also keeping in mind your desired quilt size), choose a size for either the block, the smallest patch, the largest patch, or some other particular patch. List it here as 1 graph square = _____ inches in your full-sized quilt.

Drawing the Quilt to Scale 16

By now, you have worked out a pattern sketch (perhaps with border ideas), determined a desired quilt size, and chosen a scale for your drawing. The next step is to make a drawing of the entire quilt in order to work out the details, to anticipate any problems, and to see just what the quilt will look like and how it will measure up.

Start with the desired quilt size (in inches). Divide the quilt width by the number of inches one graph square equals in your chosen scale. Do the same for the quilt length. The resulting figures are the number of graph squares across and down your drawing should cover.

Outline this area on your graph paper. This outline represents the boundaries of your desired quilt size.

Referring to your border plans, mark another outline within the first set to indicate tentative borders to scale.

Now, start drawing your quilt pattern within the inner outlines. Draw the pattern, including unit blocks and sashes or alternate blocks, if any. Fill the area as closely as possible without spoiling the symmetry of the design. Designs of alternate blocks look best with four corners alike; to achieve this you will need to plan your quilt with an odd number of blocks both across and down.

The pattern may not fill your outlined area exactly. If not, you can adjust the borders to achieve the desired quilt dimensions, or you can make the quilt a slightly different size from your original plans.

Count the number of graph squares the pattern actually covers, add the number of squares intended for borders, and multiply by the scale to figure how the dimensions will change. If the new size will provide satisfactory drop and tuck for your purposes, fill in borders to complete the quilt plan. (Some final adjustments may be necessary to fit the borders to the central pattern.)

Example. Let's continue working out the quilt plan for our example quilt. The desired quilt size (from page 111) is 74″ × 88″. Our chosen scale (from page 113) is 1 square = $1\frac{1}{2}$″. Dividing the quilt width by the scale we find that our drawing should be $49\frac{1}{3}$ squares across (74 ÷ $1\frac{1}{2}$ = $49\frac{1}{3}$). Dividing the required length by the scale, we find that the drawing should cover $58\frac{2}{3}$ squares in length (88 ÷ $1\frac{1}{2}$ = $58\frac{2}{3}$). We will outline, then, an area on graph paper $49\frac{1}{3}$ squares wide by $58\frac{2}{3}$ squares long.

Referring to our border plan (sketched with the blocks on page 113), we see that our borders are 5 graph squares wide, so we mark another outline 5 graph squares in from the first outline, as in the following illustration.

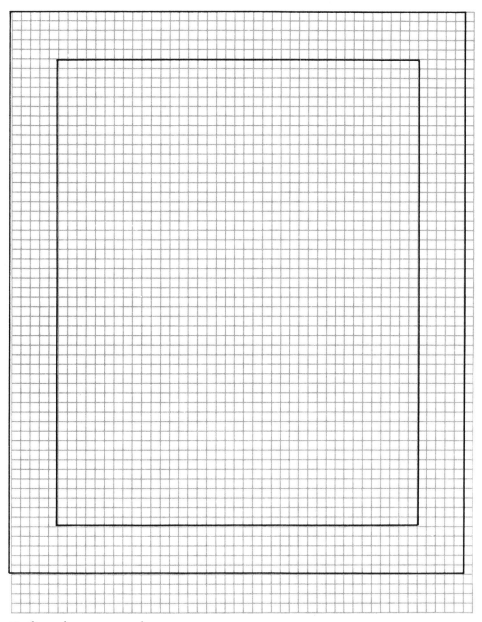

Outlines drawn on graph paper

Next, we draw the quilt to scale within the inner outlines. This is done in the next example (page 116). Notice that in order to complete the blocks around the edges our drawing is ⅔ square wider than the outlined area, and it is ⅔ square shorter. That is, the pattern actually covers 40 × 48 squares instead of 39⅓ × 48⅔ squares, as outlined.

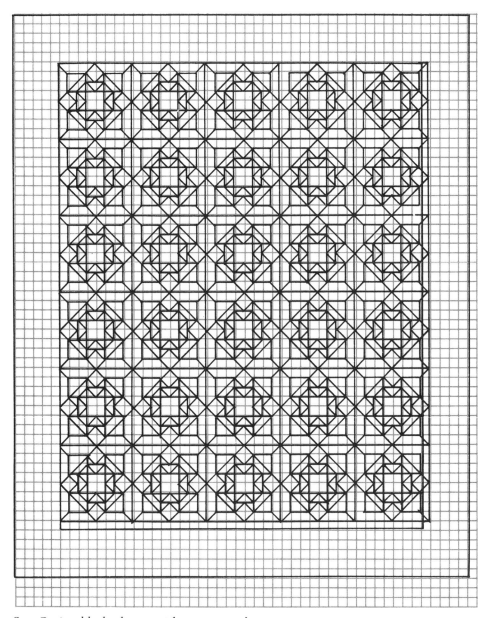

Star Gazing blocks drawn within inner outline

This is not exactly our desired quilt size, but will it be satisfactory? Adding the 5 squares on each side for borders, we determine that our quilt with borders would cover 50 × 58 squares (40 + 5 + 5 = 50; 48 + 5 + 5 = 58). Multiplying by the scale of 1 square = 1½", our actual quilt dimensions will be 75" × 87" (50 × 1½ = 75; 58 × 1½ = 87). Our actual quilt is just one inch shorter and one inch wider than our desired quilt size, so we decide to go along with it.

We draw our borders around the blocks and color the design to complete our quilt plan.

EXERCISE

Free Play. Follow these steps to draw your quilt pattern to scale.

THE SCALE DRAWING

1. On line A below list the desired quilt size (width and length).
2. On line B list the number of inches one square represents in your scale (1 square = _____ inches).
3. Divide B into A—separately for length and width—to find the number of graph squares across and down your scale drawing should cover (C).
4. On graph paper, outline the area indicated on line C. This is a representation to scale of your desired quilt size.
5. If you already know how many graph squares wide you plan to draw your borders in your scale drawing, skip to #8. If not, decide on a tentative border width and list in D.
6. List scale (same as on line B) on line E.
7. Divide D by E to find the number of squares wide your border will cover in your scale drawing, and list on line F.
8. Within the area outlined in #4 above, outline the borders. That is, draw another outline the correct number of squares (from line F) in from the outline of the desired quilt size.
9. Within the inner outline, draw your quilt design to scale, including unit blocks and set pieces, if any. Fill the area as closely as possible without spoiling the symmetry of the design.
10. The pattern may not fill your outlined area exactly. If it does not, you may adjust the border size in order to more closely approximate your ideal quilt size. Alternatively, revise your plan to make the actual quilt size either slightly larger or slightly smaller than you originally planned. (If your border is pieced, you will probably have to modify the actual size of the quilt in order to fit the border to the rest of the quilt top in a natural and attractive manner. See the discussion of pieced borders in Chapter 13.)
11. Draw the border details and color the design to complete the scale drawing.

NUMBER OF SQUARES TO OUTLINE ON GRAPH

		WIDTH	LENGTH
A.	Quilt size:	_____ inches	_____ inches
B.	Scale:	÷ _____ squares/inch	÷ _____ squares/inch
C.	Equals:	= _____ squares across	by _____ squares down

NUMBER OF SQUARES WIDE TO MAKE BORDERS

D.	Border width _____ inches
E.	Scale: ÷ _____ squares/inch
F.	Equals: = _____ squares wide

5. X-O-X-O-X (HUGS AND KISSES) 1980 96″ × 113″ This quilt was made from strips. The central motif combines elements of the traditional patterns Evening Star, Trip Around the World, and Irish Chain. The design is very much like a Single Irish Chain with Evening Stars and miniature Trip Around the World motifs alternately filling the spaces between the chains. The chains are a bit irregular, with the introduction of rectangles necessary to fit the Evening Stars. The setting is in an overall pattern with a relatively small central design area and wide pieced borders.

The central design is unusual in that it has irregular edges. Several rows of staggered squares make up the first border, which emphasizes the jagged edges of the center design. A second border of solid-colored strips undulates around the first border. The lines of the quilt center are continued in this second border, but the squares are elongated. Furthermore, the prints are eliminated in the border, which uses only the lightest shades in the quilt. The colors here grade very subtly. The combination of effects provides relief from the more active center. A third border reintroduces the prints in cameos of the central motif that fit into the border contours. Finally, a dark border squares off the edges of the quilt.

6. WHEEL OF FORTUNE   1978   96″ × 96″   The unit block in this quilt is a traditional Wheel of Fortune block. The block was interpreted in four fabrics rather than the usual two. The block size was planned around the octagon needed to suit the navy print with carefully centered nosegays.

A setting of pieced sashing in a traditional Wild Goose Chase pattern accents the triangles in the unit blocks. To hold it all together visually, plain sashing strips separate the pieced strips from the blocks. A tiny floral stripe in the plain sashes adds definition. The setting squares are pieced in two different patterns to continue the direction of the triangles in the adjacent sashing.

The pieced border repeats the sashing motif, but without the interruption of the setting squares. The unbroken ring of triangles all facing the same direction finishes the edge of the quilt emphatically.

7. BARRISTER'S BLOCK 1979 97″ × 97″   The unit block is a traditional Barrister's Block interpreted in five fabrics instead of the more typical two.

   The block is asymmetrical, so by changing the block orientation in the quilt setting, many different designs are possible. These blocks were set with narrow sashing in a simple floral stripe. Blocks were arranged tilting to the right in one row and to the left in the next row.

   A triple sawtooth border was designed from the two different-sized triangles in the block. Two of the fabrics used in the block were repeated in the border, and two new fabrics were introduced. The regrouping of the pattern elements and the slight change of color in the border make an effective frame for the quilt.

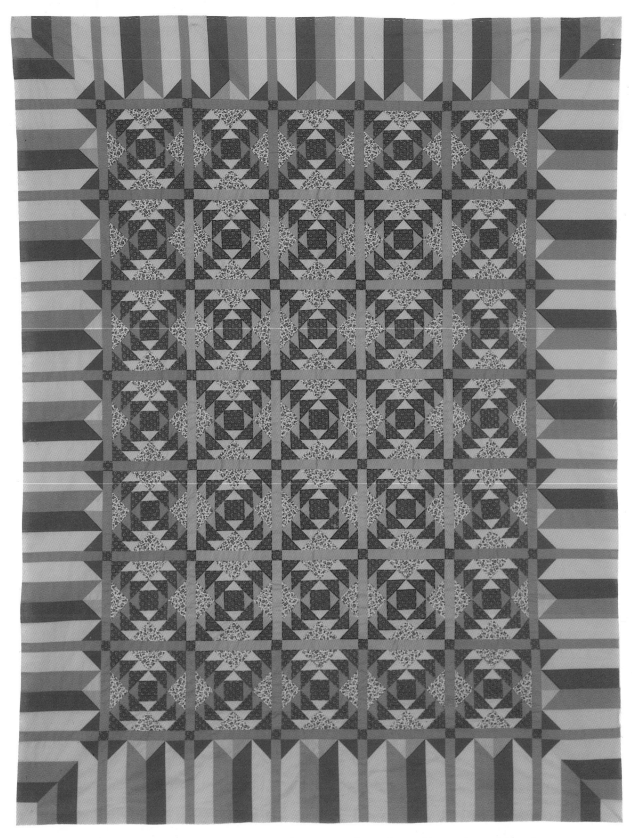

8. GREENPEACE 1979 62″ × 80″ The unit block is a traditional Rambler with a subtle color variation: Two slightly different shades of the solid fabric were used to add depth to the block. Blocks were set with sashing of squares and strips. The sashing is narrow and unobtrusive and appears to float over the quilt like beaded netting. The quilt progresses from mostly grayed green in the middle to decidedly blue. The inner border was achieved simply by changing the coloring of the unit blocks around the perimeter. The outer border has an altogether different feeling, with a change in pattern and the elimination of the green as well as the use of solids. This border was designed by extending lines from each point along the edges of the quilt.

9. HOPSCOTCH **1978** **96″ × 96″** The center of this quilt comprises two Nine Patch blocks of different colorings. They were set on the diagonal and framed with additional bands of squares. Printed bouquets and stripes were used for special effects. Since the quilt center is fairly uniform and repetitious, the border was designed to demand attention. Variable Star blocks set on the diagonal encircle the quilt. The Variable Stars were made from squares and triangles related to those in the center of the quilt. Still, in order for the blocks to fit the quilt center and go around the corners gracefully, it was necessary to insert plain strips between the border and quilt center.

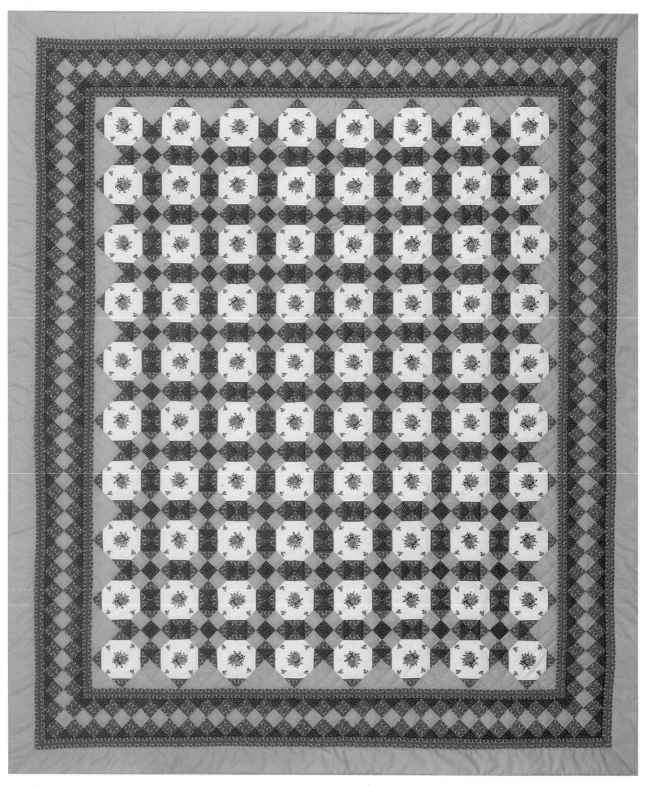

10. MAY FESTIVAL 1978 76″ × 89″ The unit block is a traditional Shoo Fly with the coloring changed to emphasize the cross shape. The green- and red-print triangles are equally dark to provide a uniform background for the gold crosses without introducing any light accents to compete with the bright white in the accessory blocks.

The Shoo Fly blocks were set alternately with Snowball accessory blocks, also traditional and based on a Nine Patch format for compatibility. The triangles around the edges of both blocks work together to form an overall pattern that is much more interesting than the individual blocks. The diagonal setting further minimizes the block boundaries.

The pieced borders incorporate the same squares and triangles used in the blocks, but they were regrouped and their color concentration is different. Plain strips were used to make the borders go around the quilt blocks with fluid corners.

11. LOG CABIN RAINBOWS 1981 66″ × 88″ Traditional Log Cabin blocks in two sizes and several different shadings of rainbow colors were arranged in a Barn Raising set. The innermost light ring of the Barn Raising is interrupted by an arrangement of thirty-two smaller blocks set in Sunshine and Shadows groupings. Blocks were colored differently to form a progression from light in the center to dark around the edges of the quilt. All solid colors were used so that the gradation of color could be smooth and free of distracting accent colors.

12. GREEN MOUNTAIN STAR   1982   63″ × 63″   The unit block is original; it combines elements of the traditional patterns Northumberland Star and David and Goliath. Each block was framed with plain green stripes with squares in the corners, then these block units were set with sashing pieced of hanging squares to echo the squares in the blocks. Gold squares at the intersections of the pieced sashes combine with the neighboring patches to form stars between the blocks. The sashing continues outside the last row of blocks to form a pieced border. A narrow plain border serves as a frame and completes the quilt.

EIGHT

Patterns and Templates

Once you have worked out all the details of your quilt design in your scale drawing, you are ready to start the process of making the quilt. First, you will need to draft full-sized patterns. Then, before you can do any marking and cutting of your fabric, you must make sturdy templates.

Drafting Full-Sized Patterns 17

Drafting the full-sized pattern pieces is just another way of drawing the block on graph paper. Use a single sheet of graph paper that is large enough to accommodate your block, or tape sheets of graph paper together, being careful to align the squares both horizontally and vertically.

To draft the patterns, start by using a pencil to mark the paper into a grid of large squares to correspond to your chosen scale. If your scale is 1 square = 2", pencil in a grid of 2" squares as shown on the following page. If your scale is 1 square = 3", pencil in a grid of 3" squares, and so forth. Count graph squares or use a ruler to measure the intervals. Ignoring the graph lines that fall *between* the lines of your *penciled* grid, copy your block square by square and line by line onto the full-sized grid. When you have copied all the lines in your block, your pattern is complete. You can make border patches or sashes and setting pieces by copying them onto the same kind of enlarged grid.

Most blocks have several patches that are the same. Since you will need only one pattern piece for each shape and size of patch, it is not usually necessary to draft the entire block on your full-sized grid. Often, ¼ of the block (or some other portion) contains all the necessary pattern pieces. You can count the squares needed for that portion of the block, outline the area, and copy just the desired part of the block, line by line and square by square.

Example. In order to draft the full-sized pattern pieces for our example quilt in Plate 1 and on page 113, we start by marking our graph paper into a grid of large squares to correspond to our chosen scale. Our scale, you will recall, is 1 square = 1½", so we mark a grid of 1½" squares on our graph paper. Then we simply copy onto the enlarged grid enough of the block to include at least one of every shape and size of pattern piece needed. The border in this example uses the same pattern pieces as the block, so that all we have to draw is what is shown in the second illustration here.

As you gain experience in drafting full-sized patterns, you may find that you no longer need to pencil in the grid of large squares. Instead, you can use ruler and graph squares to imagine where the enlarged squares would be as you copy your block or partial block to make full-sized pattern pieces.

Grid of 2″ squares

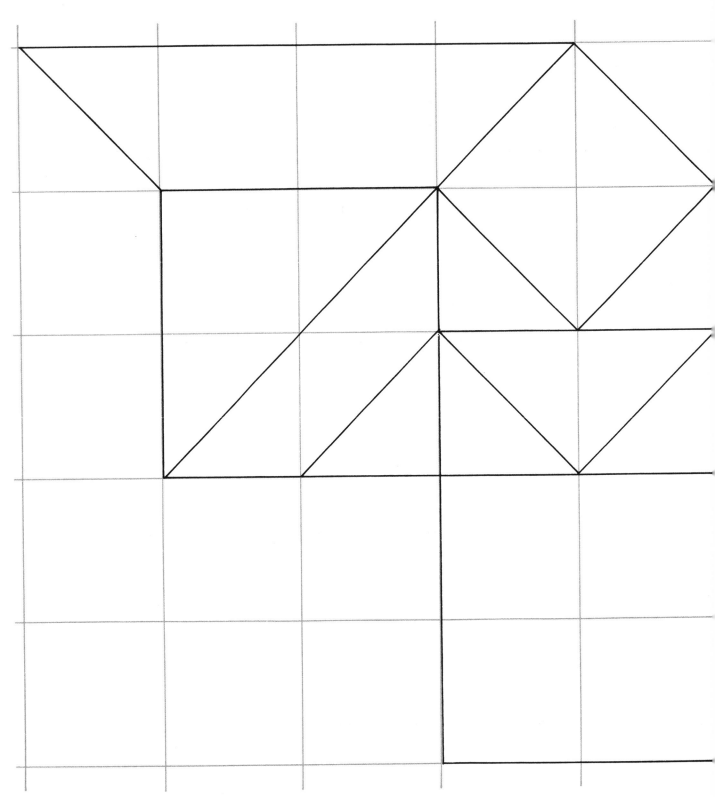

Star Gazing patterns drafted full size on 1½" grid

EXERCISE

DRAFTING THE PATTERN PIECES

Free Play. Use the following procedure to draw your full-sized patterns.

1. Refer to the scale of your quilt plan: 1 square = _____ inches. With a pencil, draw a grid of squares this size superimposed on graph paper.
2. Ignoring the blue graph lines and following your penciled grid, copy your block (or enough of the block to contain every type of patch) square by square and line by line to make the full-sized patterns.

Making Templates 18

The pattern pieces that you have just drawn represent the pieces of the unit block as they will appear in the finished quilt. In practical terms, you have just drawn the stitching lines of the patches. If you plan to make your quilt using traditional methods, you will want to mark these stitching lines onto each patch of fabric to guide you in cutting and sewing the quilt. In order to transfer the stitching lines onto the fabric, you need to make a template. This is a fairly stiff and sturdy version of the pattern piece that you hold in place on the fabric and mark around with a pencil or tailor's chalk.

Making Traditional Templates for Hand Sewing. Simply mount the graph paper pattern drawing on a piece of tagboard or cardboard, using a glue stick or rubber cement, or trace the pattern onto clear template plastic. Then cut out the templates for the individual patches along the drawn lines. The following illustration shows a template for hand sewing.

The actual patches of fabric will be cut out with ¼" seam allowances added outside the marked stitching lines. These seam allowances can be added to the patches by eye as you mark and cut the fabric, or you can make a window template to mark both cutting line and stitching line of each patch.

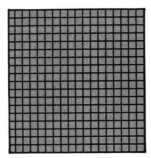

Hand-sewing template

Making Window Templates. Cut out the individual pattern pieces of your full-sized graph drawing. Carefully trace around each separate pattern piece on cardboard, tagboard, or template plastic, leaving enough room around each pattern to add seam allowances. Measure and mark cutting lines ¼" outside the traced stitching lines. Cut out along both cutting lines and stitching lines. Each template will be a narrow ring with a large hole in the middle as in the example here.

Window template

Making Templates for Machine Sewing. Marked seam lines are not necessary for piecing on the sewing machine. As in dressmaking, you simply use a mark on the sewing-machine throat plate to gauge your seam line an even distance from the cut edge of the fabric. For this reason, it is very important to cut the patches for machine sewing very accurately. To do this you will need to make templates with precise $\frac{1}{4}''$ seam allowances already included, as follows.

Cut out the individual pattern pieces of your full-sized graph drawing, and trace around each piece on cardboard, tagboard, or template plastic. Leave space around each piece to add seam allowances, just as you would for window templates. Measure and mark cutting lines precisely $\frac{1}{4}''$ outside the stitching lines. Cut out the template on the outer line only. The following illustration shows a template for machine sewing.

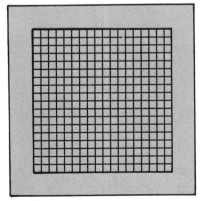

Machine-sewing template

Whether you make window templates or templates for hand or machine sewing, it will be helpful to mark each shape with the colors and quantitites you will need to cut for your quilt. If you plan to save your templates for possible reuse later, store them in an envelope along with a block sketch to refresh your memory.

EXERCISE

MAKING TEMPLATES

Free Play. Decide on a construction technique (hand or machine sewing), and choose the appropriate kind of template. Then make templates for your unit block as described in either 1, 2, or 3.

1. Standard templates for hand sewing. Mount your pattern drawing onto something stiff like cardboard, or trace the pattern drawing onto clear plastic. Cut apart to make templates for the individual shapes.
2. Window templates. Cut out the graphed pattern drawing around each patch. Trace around the patches onto cardboard or plastic, leaving room to measure and mark $\frac{1}{4}''$ seam allowances around each one. Cut out on both the outer cutting line and the inner stitching line to complete window templates.
3. Sewing-machine templates. Cut out the individual patches of your pattern drawing. Trace around the patches onto cardboard or plastic, leaving space around the patches for seam allowances. Measure and mark cutting lines $\frac{1}{4}''$ outside the stitching lines. Cut out on the outer lines only.

NINE

Fabrics

Interpreting your quilt drawing in fabrics requires design decisions as well as considerations of a more practical nature. Once you have made these decisions, you'll be ready to purchase yardage or select from your fabric on hand. To do this successfully requires some understanding of yardage estimation. The following lessons will help you with the decisions and figuring involved in translating your quilt plan into fabrics.

Selecting Materials 19

Practical Considerations. In general, yardage and scraps should be colorfast, firmly woven, and have plenty of body. Avoid limp or stretchy fabrics, as they lose their shape with handling. Avoid loosely woven fabrics or those with a tendency to unravel. Remember that seam allowances are a mere ¼″ in patchwork, so there is not much leeway for raveling. It is generally wise to use similar types and weights of fabrics in a bed quilt. You have more flexibility in fabric selection for a wall quilt, as wear and laundering are not major considerations.

Some fabrics or combinations may present problems to the inexperienced quilter. For example, slick fabrics like satin and pile fabrics such as velvet may slip out of place as you stitch; heavy fabrics such as corduroy may prove bulky at the seams and impossible to quilt.

Cottons and cotton blends are admirably suited to patchwork. Many quilters insist on 100% cotton, although an occasional blend of at least 65% cotton is not objectionable. Most of the new 100% cottons have a permanent-press finish which greatly improves laundering performance of the quilt. Calico, chintz, and broadcloth are ideal.

Small prints, calicoes, dots, florals, and gingham checks are among the favorite patterns for use in quilts. Especially with small, regularly spaced prints, it is important that the print be on grain. Fabrics with permanent-press finish cannot be stretched to correct the grain, so what you see on the bolt is what you get. Checks larger than about ¼″ should be avoided, as they exaggerate any irregularity of the fabric, the cutting, or the stitching. Foulard-type prints, paisleys, splashy florals, and stripes can be used successfully if chosen carefully. Prints that are widely spaced on the background appear plain in small patchwork pieces unless each patch is carefully cut with the printed motif centered in it. Stripes require special attention in cutting, but the results often justify the extra work involved. Large prints can be incoherent in small patches, with each patch appearing to be made of a different fabric. However, large prints with fine detail or fairly uniform color can be used to advantage in patchwork.

Batting is available from most fabric stores, quilt stores, and mail-order quilting supply sources. Batting comes in sheet form, folded and rolled up like a sleeping bag. When you buy your batting, make sure that you can see from the end of the package that it is rolled. Otherwise you may mistake simple stuffing for batting; it is not always clearly labeled. Stuffing is not in sheet form and is no substitute for batting. Quilt batting typically comes in dimensions of 72″ or 80″ × 90″. Larger sizes are available from some sources, or small batts can be spliced together for large quilts. Upholstery stores often sell batting by the yard in 45″ widths suitable for splicing.

Batting is available in cotton, polyester fiber, or a blend of the two. Most modern quilters use the polyester batting, as it is more lightweight, launders beautifully, and does not have to be quilted as closely as the cotton variety. Quality varies widely from brand to brand in polyester batts. Quality and price are not invariably related, but it is wise to avoid the cheapest batts, as they tend to be uneven and far too delicate to withstand normal handling. It is largely a matter of personal taste whether you select a batt with a hard, glazed finish or a soft finish. Both feel soft in the finished quilt. The glazed batts are significantly easier to work with, and they are less likely to beard or lose fibers through the weave of the fabric. On the other hand, the soft-finished batts seem to retain their body better with laundering. I recommend the glazed batts for quilting and the soft-finished ones for tied comforters. For especially thick comforters, two-pound batts are sometimes available. Alternatively, you can layer two (or more) one-pound batts to produce the same effect with just a little more work.

Any standard sewing thread will do to piece the quilt top. Use cotton or cotton-wrapped polyester as your custom dictates. Use white thread or thread matching the lightest color in the quilt. You may as well buy the largest spool you can find because the typical bed quilt requires six to ten refills of the bobbin (or at least 300 yards of thread) for machine sewing.

Quilt shops and fabric stores carry quilting thread in a variety of weights and fibers. Experiment to find the thread that best suits you. Some quilters even use regular sewing thread for the quilting. Choose thread for quilting in a color that blends well with the various colors in the quilt top. The quilting is usually done in one thread color only. Most often, quilting is done in white or off-white; sometimes the quilting thread is chosen to match the lining fabric.

If you plan to tie your comforter with yarn, the yarn should be washable and sufficiently fine to pose no problem in penetrating all layers of the quilt and batting. Orlon baby yarn and sport-weight or fingering yarn are ideal. Three-ply yarn is less likely to unravel than two-ply. For less conspicuous ties, use buttonhole twist or heavy carpet thread. Avoid embroidery floss, as it is slippery and tends to untie itself even when double knotted.

Design Considerations. Your drawing will define the number of colors in your quilt and their relationships to each other (whether contrasting or close shades of the same hue, for example). However, the drawing is a mere suggestion of what the finished quilt will look like. You probably didn't draw prints (and even if you did, they could only hint at the complexity of real patterned fabrics). Your drawing lacks the texture and the depth added by accent colors that are incidental to printed fabrics. It also lacks the rich and subtle blending of colors in a print and the dancing effect of small-scale and large-scale prints working in concert in an actual quilt.

Selecting fabrics to translate your drawing into a quilt that is warm and real is one of the most creative, enjoyable, and important parts of the design process. Even at this stage of the quilt design, you will have many options, and the character of your quilt depends on your decisions.

You can choose splashy prints or all solid colors for a modern appearance; you can choose earth tones and nubbly textures for an organic look; you can go elegant with glittery lamé, shimmering satins, and rich velvets; or you can achieve a quaint, traditional effect with cotton calicoes.

Your fabric selection decisions are important, but I say this to excite, not to intimidate you. The choices are not difficult; they are a matter of personal taste. Simply choose what appeals to you, and you can't go wrong. If you are a beginner, unaccustomed to putting prints and textures together for a quilt, you may not be sure about what you want, so here are a few suggestions to consider.

Study your colored quilt plan. Do the colors and arrangement seem more suited to a traditional or modern treatment? Is it already busy, or could it use the kind of enlivening that prints add?

In what context will the quilt be used? Are you counting on the quilt to give an old-fashioned, homey touch to a room? Or would a strikingly modern piece provide a spark of the unexpected that suits your purpose?

What kind of quilts do you like? Do you find yourself drawn consistently to the scrap variety? Do you gravitate toward the really innovative, contemporary ones? Or are you more comfortable with pleasant, middle-of-the-road quilts made from a few well-coordinated prints and solids?

What kinds of fabrics are you comfortable working with? Broadcloth-weight cottons are the easiest to handle. Heavy fabrics, limp ones, sheer or stretchy ones can present some problems you'd rather not have to contend with.

Do you plan to do a lot of quilting? Better stick to lightweights such as cotton broadcloth. Will the quilt receive much wear and tear? Use fabrics that won't ravel, shrink, bleed, or wrinkle unduly—and make sure they are compatible for laundering purposes. (Reading the care instructions on the bolt will give you some clues; only prewashing will provide a true test of a fabric's performance, though.) If your quilt will be used as a decorative wall hanging, feel free to choose from the wide range of fibers and textures available with less regard for launderability.

Do you want a sedate or tranquil look? Find a print that has all the colors of the quilt, in however small doses. It will unify the quilt by reiterating the color scheme. Repetition is very comfortable; try using the same fabrics in the same positions in each block for a very calming effect. Use solids both as relief from the prints and for definition of shapes to make the quilt less confusing.

Would you rather have your quilt dance and shimmer? Use color tension—complementary colors, slightly clashing or mismatched shades, or unexpected accents to enliven the surface. Alternatively, use many prints of different scales and values or a multitude of scrap prints for sparkle. Or use the play of light on smooth and rough textures to provide interest.

If you have paired a silk blouse with a wool skirt and an angora sweater (or a corduroy skirt with an oxford-cloth shirt and leather loafers), you've had experience combining textures. Textures are combined in many areas of our lives—not only in clothing, but also in home furnishings and on the dinner plate, to name a few. If you haven't made a quilt, you probably don't have experience in combining different prints, though. Therefore, I'd like to discuss this subject in more detail.

Whatever color scheme you choose, it is important to remember considerations of contrast when combining prints. Most patchwork designs call for strong contrast between at least two of the fabrics. Without contrast, the pattern fades. Suppose you decide on bright yellow and dark brown. These colors are, themselves, highly contrasting. Still, what we might call a yellow print and a brown print may not contrast much at all in certain circumstances. A small brown dot on a white background appears almost white. A yellow floral print widely spaced on a white background also appears white. The contrast is minimal. For purposes of color contrast in patchwork, it is generally the background color that is critical. If the pattern is quite closely spaced, the basic color of the figure gains importance. The best way to determine what color a print will appear is to squint at it or look at it in the mirror.

There is more to contrast than just color. Two splotchy prints with designs of similar sizes and spacing will blend together when placed side by side, in spite of contrasting colors. The visual texture is important here. The term "visual texture" refers to the nature of the pattern—whether splotchy, splashy, systematically repetitive, sparse, or busy. It also refers to the quality of the detail—whether delicate, complex, bold, or blurred. To judge the visual texture of a fabric, the squint test is, once again, helpful. Squinting will minimize color differences, allowing you to concentrate on the patterns.

The cardinal rule for successfully combining prints is to avoid too much of the same thing. A varied visual texture with a comfortable balance of pattern and relief makes a quilt interesting without bombarding the senses.

Some people seem to have a knack for selecting fabrics that work well together. If you do not yet feel confident in your ability to do so, try using one or two regular, rhythmic prints and a solid along with each principal fabric in your quilt.

The principal fabric is so called because it provides the color scheme for the quilt. The print can portray anything from creeping vines to dancing bears. Whatever the subject, it is rendered in some detail and depth of color.

The regular, rhythmic prints are not as interesting as the principal fabrics, but they do offer some textural interest. These are simple prints, usually of just two or three colors. Dots, calicoes, checks, stripes, and other small, uniformly spaced, regularly repeated patterns fit this classification. The visual effect of such patterns derives mostly from the rhythm of the spacing. Too much of the same rhythm can be boring. I don't advise using two checks of a similar size together, for instance. Regular prints of different rhythms, such as a small dot and a differently spaced calico, can work well together.

Plain colors often complement an array of prints. Solid colors offer relief from the patterned fabrics and give definition to the shapes. Plain colors used to the exclusion of prints tend to produce a crisp, modern effect.

The placement of each fabric within the quilt design should take into account factors of color contrast and visual texture. High contrast is probably most critical between figure and background. Grading of color within the figure is suggested by some unit blocks, but at least moderate contrast is essential for the design to emerge. Aside from the considerations of contrast, placement is largely a matter of personal taste.

The principal fabric need not be reserved for the major figure elements of the quilt. It may act as a receding color more suited to the background of the unit block. Traditionally, sashing and alternate blocks were cut from solid-color fabrics. This was done, as often as not, to provide a suitable space to show off fine quilting. Plain-colored set pieces tend to look formal. White looks especially old-fashioned. You may want to give your quilt added character with patterned set pieces.

Where your design calls for neighboring patches to be made from the same fabric, it is best to avoid using prints that are very rhythmic and evenly spaced. Instead, use solids or, better yet, use splashy prints that will obscure the seam lines.

These guidelines are not entirely applicable to scrap quilts. Still, scrap quilts need not be random. Consideration of textural variety and color contrast in adjacent patches can make your scrap quilt something out of the ordinary. If you have great quantities of scraps, you might even consider restricting your fabrics to a limited range of colors—warm fall tones, for example—for an exceptionally handsome quilt.

Yardage Estimation and Cutting Layouts 20

Having planned your quilt design so carefully, you will want to make sure you have sufficient yardage to complete the quilt as planned. If you are buying all new materials, it is a simple matter of figuring how much you need to buy. However, the prettiest quilts are often made from fabrics collected over the years. And if you buy ahead with no particular quilt in mind, how much should you buy? Generally, a two-yard length will be enough for one of the main fabrics in a quilt made from just a few fabrics. Buy three yards if you think you'll use the fabric for borders or long sashes. One and one-half yards will suffice for an accent fabric for almost any quilt. Buy nine yards if the fabric is a real bargain—you can make a pretty lining from it for less than the cost of a plain lining. If you really love a fabric and think you'll use it again and again, buy as much as your budget (and closet space) will allow. I seldom buy quarter-yard and eighth-yard lengths unless I need to fill out my scrap collection for a specific project. Even then, I prefer to buy at least a half-yard because I hate to use the last bit of any fabric, and these small bits simply get used up too fast for my liking. Anyway, if I've bought a quarter-yard, I'll surely decide that the fabric is the only possible one to use for a project requiring twice that amount. Then I'll end up pulling my hair out trying to find more at the store or cajoling a friend into parting with her last bit of it.

Most quilters don't mind having leftover fabric. If you've got the money to spend on extra fabric, you can save yourself the trouble of figuring yardage requirements—for a while at least. Eventually, though, you'll whittle your supplies down to the point where you'll want to know whether or not there is enough to complete your current project.

Making a Cutting Requirements Chart. Figuring yardage requires some arithmetic. It's pretty much common sense, but if the idea of math intimidates you, perhaps you can convince a dear friend, your husband (or wife), or one of your talented children to do the figuring for you. Whether you do the figuring yourself or have it done for you, you'll need to start by making a cutting requirements chart. This simply lists each fabric and the type and number of patches to be cut from it.

Start your cutting requirements chart by making a column for each fabric in the quilt. Along the left side of the chart make a row for each shape and size of patch. Include sashing, alternate blocks, border strips, and lining as well as patches. Use your scale drawing and full-sized patterns to determine dimensions for the pieces. Remember to allow for $\frac{1}{4}''$ seams. Referring to your colored quilt plan, count the number needed of each piece for each fabric, and enter it on your chart. The chart shows the cutting requirements for the quilt (Plate 1) which we have been using in our examples.

CUTTING REQUIREMENTS CHART FOR EXAMPLE QUILT (Plate 1)
Number of Pieces Needed of Each Shape, Size, and Color

PATCHES	GOLD	RUST PRINT	RUST SOLID	OLIVE	LIGHT PRINT	BROWN	NAVY	LIGHT STRIPE
Lining Panel 40″ × 91″	2							
Border Strip 2″ × 89″			2					
Border Strip 2″ × 77″			2					
Large Square 3½″	30							
Large Trapezoid 2″ × 5″ × 6½″	52					168	168	
Small Trapezoid 1⅝″ × 2⅝″ × 4¾″								120
Large Triangle 2 in 3⅞″ square					120			
Small Square 2⅝″	44		22		142			
Medium Triangle 2 in 3″ square	52	120	96					
Small Triangle 2 in 2⅜″ square	240	240		120				

Cutting Layouts. After you have determined what you will need to cut from each fabric, you must plan cutting layouts to figure out the yardage needed of each fabric. Consider the different fabrics one at a time. Sketch a rectangular shape representing an unknown length of fabric 44″ wide (or 36″ wide, depending on what you have or plan to buy). Mark off the space needed for the large pieces first. Figure out how much of the fabric width remains for cutting smaller patches, and how many patches will fit in a row. Mark off the number of rows needed, listing dimensions of each row. When you have marked off all the pattern pieces needed from that fabric, add up the dimensions to see the number of inches of fabric needed. Divide by 36 to find the number of yards. Allow a little extra for shrinkage and cutting error. Repeat for each fabric in the quilt. Cutting layouts for two of the fabrics in our cover example quilt are shown in the following illustrations.

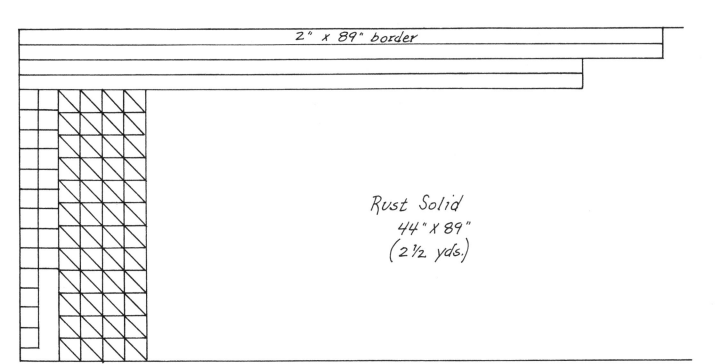

Rust Solid
44" x 89"
(2½ yds.)

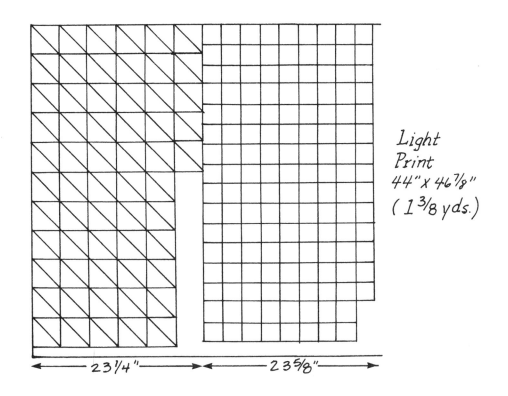

Light
Print
44" x 46⅞"
(1 ⅜ yds.)

EXERCISE   Free Play.

**YARDAGE
ESTIMATION AND
CUTTING LAYOUTS**

1. Fill out the cutting requirements chart given for your quilt design. For each column head describe one of the fabrics you will be using. In the column labeled "Patches" list the different shapes and sizes of pieces needed. Don't forget borders and lining. Include seam allowances in the dimensions. Referring to your quilt plan, count the number needed of each patch in each color, and list in the appropriate space in the chart that follows.

CUTTING REQUIREMENTS CHART
Number of Pieces Needed of Each Shape, Size, and Color

PATCHES (Shape and Dimensions)	FABRIC #1	FABRIC #2	FABRIC #3	FABRIC #4	FABRIC #5	FABRIC #6	FABRIC #7	FABRIC #8

2. Make a cutting layout for each fabric listed in your cutting requirements chart. Make a sketch representing a length of 44″ wide (or 36″ wide) fabric. Mark off the space needed to cut large patches, then smaller ones. Figure out how many patches will fit in a row, and mark off the number of rows needed. List dimensions of the rows, and add up the measurements to figure the total yardage needed of each fabric.

Fabric Preparation 21

If you ever plan to launder the finished quilt, you will want to be confident that the fabrics will not shrink, fade, or bleed color. Therefore, before you invest a great deal of time in cutting, piecing, and quilting, it would be wise to spend a few minutes prewashing the fabrics. Start by immersing one fabric at a time in a few inches of tap water in the sink. Use a temperature comparable to that which you plan to use when laundering the finished quilt. Squeeze the water through the fabric gently. If the water remains clear after a few squeezes, put the wet fabric aside, and immerse the next fabric. If the color runs and discolors the water, hold the fabric under running water, squeezing gently until you think that the color is through bleeding. Rinse the sink, refill, and immerse the fabric again. If the water remains clear, put the fabric aside and continue testing other fabrics. If the water discolors again, continue rinsing until the water is clear. Occasionally, you may want to put a single problem fabric through a cycle in your automatic washer, then test again in the sink to make sure it is through bleeding color. Rarely, you may encounter a fabric that refuses to stop bleeding color. Put it aside for a project that you don't expect to launder, or get rid of it.

When all the fabrics test as colorfast, put them in your automatic washer, and launder as you will the quilt. (I use warm water and detergent on the permanent-press setting, then a cool rinse.) Tumble dry. (Quilts should not be line dried, as the weight of the wet batting may put too much stress on the quilting stitches and cause tearing.)

Press the fabrics. If you don't plan to start marking and cutting immediately, you might prefer to put off ironing the fabrics until you are ready to begin construction. Simply smooth out any wrinkles and fold for storage.

TEN

Quilt Construction

Now that you have made your pattern templates and collected your fabrics, you are ready to start marking and cutting, then sewing and quilting. Even if you have been making quilts for years, you may want to take a look at the remaining few chapters to see if you can pick up any shortcuts or pointers that will make the construction of your quilt easier or more enjoyable. Should you seek further technical advice or inspiration, a reading list is on page 159.

Happy quilting.

Marking and Cutting

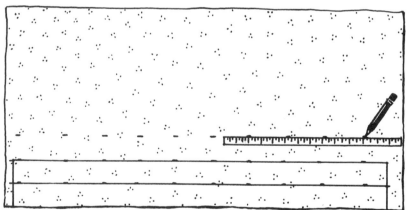

Marking and Cutting Large Straight Pieces Without Templates. Refer to your cutting requirements chart to determine the dimensions of border strips, sashing, alternate plain blocks or setting triangles, and lining pieces. These measurements include seam allowances. There is no need to make templates for these large pieces. Simply use a yardstick and pencil to measure and mark these shapes directly onto the fabric. Start by straightening the grain of the fabric. Then spread the fabric, face down, in one layer on a table, cutting board, or other clean, hard surface. Mark a ruled line ½″ from each selvage, and trim off the selvages along these lines. Use a yardstick and pencil to measure and mark length and width dimensions as listed for border strips or other large pieces. Measure the width of the piece from the trimmed edge, and make a small mark. Repeat at intervals of a foot or so for the length needed. Connect the marks with a yardstick and pencil line. Use a carpenter's square or a C-Thru® ruler to form right angles for squares or border ends. The following illustration shows how to mark border strips this way.

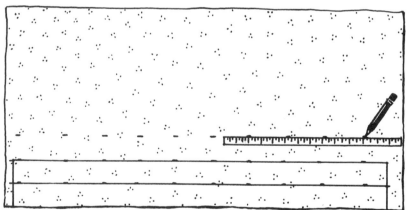

Marking border strips

If you are unsure about the accuracy of your sewing, you can cut the border strips a couple of inches longer than your design calls for. Alternatively, you can wait to cut strips until you are ready to attach them so that you can measure the actual quilt top and make borders to fit.

To mark large right triangles, mark off a square ⅞″ bigger than the finished dimension (without seam allowances) of the short sides of the triangle. Cut out the square on the marked lines. Fold the square in half diagonally, and crease.

Cut along the crease to form two triangle patches with ¼″ seam allowances included all around.

Using Standard Templates for Hand Sewing. Press the fabric. Lay it face down in a single smooth layer on a clean, dry table. Referring to your cutting layout, mark large pieces first, then smaller ones. Observe grain line as you position the templates. Wherever possible, edges of the patch should be on the lengthwise or crosswise grains. Draw around the template which you have placed face down on the wrong side of the fabric. Use a sharp lead pencil or tailor's chalk to mark, and leave ½″ between patches. Cut out, adding ¼″ seam allowances by eye to each patch.

Using Window Templates. Press the fabric, and lay it face down on the table in a single layer. Refer to your cutting layout, and observe grain line as you mark. Use a sharp lead pencil or tailor's chalk to trace around the inner edge of template to mark stitching lines and to trace around the outer edge to mark cutting lines. Mark patches with templates face down on the wrong side of the fabric and with cutting lines of neighboring patches touching wherever possible. Cut out the patches on the outer (cutting) lines.

Using Templates for Machine Sewing. Press the fabric. Fold it into as many layers as your scissors can cut through easily. (Gingher® brand scissors will cut through eight to ten layers accurately and comfortably. Other scissors may be able to handle only two to four layers.) Press each layer over the last as you fold. Refer to your cutting layout, and observe grain line as you position the template. Use a pencil or tailor's chalk to mark around the template onto the top layer of fabric only. Or, if you prefer, simply hold the template in place with your fingers as you cut right on the ironing board. Cut through all layers of fabric, being careful to hold the scissors straight so that the patch on the bottom layer is no bigger or smaller than the patch on the top layer of fabric. Cut with short strokes at the middle of the blades, not at the tip of the scissors. Cut patches close together or touching to conserve fabric and cutting strokes.

Note: If your quilt pattern calls for asymmetrical patches that all face the same direction, do not fold the fabric. (Folding results in mirror images, which are usually fine, but not in this instance.) Instead, cut the fabric into a few lengths and layer the pieces, all face down. If you prefer not to cut the fabric into lengths, you will have to cut these asymmetrical patches one at a time. Be careful to place the template face down each time you mark or cut around it.

Adapting Machine-Sewing Templates and Marking Techniques for Hand Sewing. Even if you are hand piecing, you can take advantage of this speedy cutting method. Make both a hand-sewing template and a machine-sewing template for each pattern piece. Fold and press the fabric in layers as described for the machine technique. Position one of the machine templates (with seam allowances included), mark on the top layer only, and cut (or simply hold in place and cut) through all layers of the fabric. Continue cutting all the patches in this manner. After cutting patches, center the corresponding hand-sewing template over each patch, and mark the stitching line.

Sewing Strategies 23

As you design your quilt, it is important that you have an understanding of block piecing. This will enable you to judge the practicality of your design and to plan designs suited to your level of sewing skills. It is also a good idea to map out your sewing strategy before you begin quilt construction. By planning ahead, you can avoid awkward sewing problems and make your quilt in the easiest manner possible.

Judging the Difficulty of a Pattern. Basically, difficulty can be divided into factors of time and trickiness. Getting involved in making a quilt with too great a time factor can try your patience. Choosing a project requiring skills beyond your experience can be equally frustrating. It is easy to tell if a quilt pattern will take a long time to make; simply count the pieces. Once you are familiar with a few of the indicators, you can spot a tricky piecing situation easily, too. Consider these factors when you are designing your quilt.

It is easier to sew squares and rectangles than triangles, diamonds, or other pointed patches. With squares and rectangles, you don't have to deal with stretchy bias edges. Furthermore, perfect points require precision at every seam. You can get away with a slightly deep or shallow seam when you are joining squares. It is also easier to sew stubby triangles than long, pointy ones. (If you cut the pointy patch slightly wide or narrow, the length of the point can be affected drastically.)

It is easier to achieve a perfect point alongside a plain patch than it is to align two points. (The more points you have coming together in one place, the more difficult the sewing will be.)

It is easier to make a block that can be sewn in rows than one that has to have patches inserted into odd angles.

Stitching Order. Most often, blocks are made from rows of patches. It is best to avoid stitching around corners, so if you can figure out a way to join the patches in straight rows, do so. The rows can be horizontal, vertical, or diagonal. Sometimes, patches must be joined into squares before the squares can be joined in rows. On page 151 are some examples showing how blocks are made from rows.

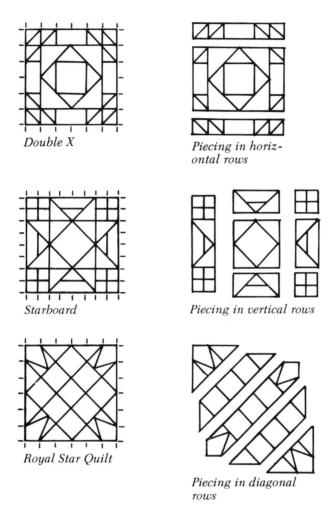

Double X

Piecing in horiz-
ontal rows

Starboard

Piecing in vertical rows

Royal Star Quilt

Piecing in diagonal
rows

Sometimes, blocks are made by starting in the center and adding patches concentrically to the sides. The Log Cabin block shown below is a good example of this.

Occasionally, blocks are made from a combination of row construction and concentric construction. Snail's Trail, on page 152, shows a block of this type. First the squares are joined in two rows of two; the triangles are then added concentrically.

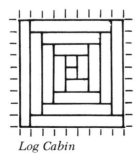

Log Cabin

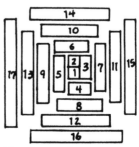

Numbers indicate piecing
order

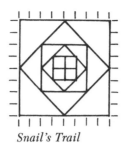

Snail's Trail

*Numbers indicate
piecing order*

As a general rule, you should always plan to sew the longest seam last. If one long patch faces a number of smaller ones, join the smaller ones before adding the long one.

When you are getting ready to make a quilt from one of your block-and-set sketches, study the pattern to work out a sewing strategy. Will the block be made in rows or concentrically? How tricky is the sewing? Occasionally, a design is pretty on paper, but it is just not practical to sew. If you decide that your design is one of these, see if you can modify the pattern to make it easier to construct. If not, it may be best to shelve this design and select another one to work on.

Sewing 24

Basic Hand-Sewing Technique. Place two patches right sides together. Stick a pin through the point marking the end of the seam line for one patch; continue through the corresponding point on the second patch. Stick another pin through the patches at the opposite end of the seam line to further align the patches. Pin to hold the patches in this position. Use a single thread, a short (#7 or #8 betweens) needle, and a small, even running stitch to join the patches along the marked lines. Sew only to the end of the seam lines, and take a couple of back stitches at both ends of the seam to secure it.

Basic Machine-Sewing Technique. You will recall that for machine stitching patches are not marked with seam lines. Instead, precise ¼″ seam allowances are added to the templates so that the patches can be cut very accurately. The seam lines simply follow ¼″ inside the cut edges of the patches. Use the edge of your presser foot as a gauge if its edge is ¼″ from the needle. If your machine has a ¼″ mark etched on the throat plate, use it as a guide. Otherwise, make your own seam guide as follows.

Cut out one of your graph-paper pattern pieces with seam allowances included. Insert the needle of your sewing machine into the seam line drawn on the paper pattern. Lower the presser foot, and stitch (with or without thread) for an inch or so to make sure that the needle is following the seam line exactly. (Raise the presser foot, and straighten the pattern if necessary.) When you are satisfied that the needle is going straight down the seam line, leave the presser foot down, and place a piece of masking tape on the throat plate of the machine directly alongside the cut edge of the pattern piece. Remove the pattern piece. Keep the patches of fabric in line with the edge of the masking tape as you stitch.

Some sewing machines have wide presser feet and feed dogs. It is difficult to gauge and sew narrow ¼″ seams on machines of this type, since you can't place a strip of tape over the feed dog. What you can do in this case is to make your seam allowances deeper than the usual ¼″. Follow this procedure.

Draw stitching lines of a pattern piece on graph paper, leaving room for seam allowances around the pattern. Don't cut out the pattern. Insert the sewing machine needle into the drawn seam line on the paper, lower the presser foot, and stitch along the seam line, adjusting as necessary until the stitching follows the drawn line exactly. With a pencil, mark a line on the graph paper right along the edge of the presser foot. Remove the pattern. Use a ruler to measure the distance from the seam line to the pencil mark indicating the presser foot location. This measurement will be the depth of your seam allowances, and the edge of the presser foot will be your sewing guide. Measure and mark seam allowances of this depth on all your pattern pieces.

For machine sewing, set your stitch length at about ten stitches per inch. Use a needle of the appropriate size for the fabric you are using, as listed on the package of needles. Choose a thread color that will not show through any of the fabrics, and wind several bobbins in advance. Place patches with right sides together and cut edges aligned. Pin long seams; pin short seams at joints only. Align the cut edges of the patches with the seam guide, and stitch from edge to edge of the patches. If it is necessary for the seam allowances to remain free, as when inserting a patch into an angle, stitch only to the ends of the seam lines (1/4" in from cut edges). Back stitch at ends of all seams.

Pressing. Be careful not to stretch bias edges out of shape when you press. Press only in the direction of the straight grain of the fabric. It is not necessary to press after each seam. You can simply finger-crease the seam allowances to one side. Press the seams toward the darker fabric wherever possible. Press seam allowances in opposite directions at a joint where several patches come together, as in the following illustration. Press the wrong side of the block first, then press the right side.

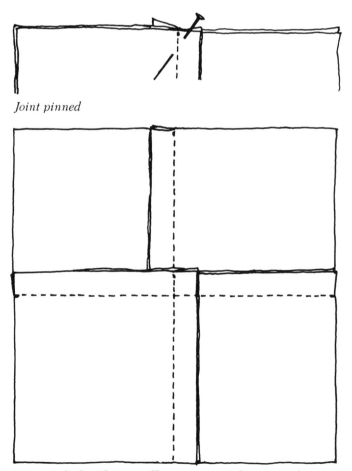

Joint pinned

Joint stitched with seam allowances turned opposite directions

Setting the Quilt Together. Make all of the blocks. Next join the blocks in rows. Finally, join the rows. If your quilt has a diagonal set, the rows of blocks will not go straight across the quilt. Instead, the rows will go diagonally across the quilt. Each row will have two more (or fewer) blocks than the last, and each row will end with setting triangles. The illustration below shows how to piece the rows of a diagonally set quilt.

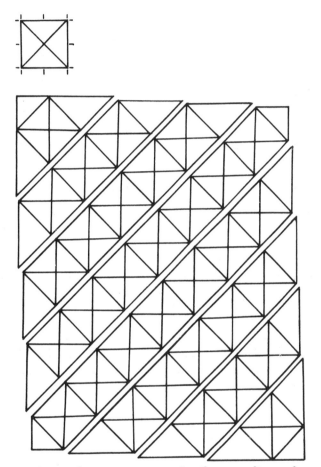

Broken Dishes, construction of quilt set on diagonal

If the quilt is set with sashing, insert short sashing strips between blocks in a row, and insert long sashes between rows of blocks. The example on page 156 illustrates the assembly of a sashed quilt.

Broken Sash, construction of quilt set with sashing

Attaching Borders. For butted borders, pin, then sew a strip to one edge of the quilt, then the opposite edge. Trim the ends even with the quilt top. Pin and sew the other two strips to the remaining edges, and trim. Attach additional borders in a similar fashion.

For mitered corners, first pin and sew together multiple border strips in sequence, matching centers. Pin and sew a set of borders to each side of the quilt, sewing only to the end of the seam lines of the quilt top and matching centers. Place the quilt face down, and smooth the borders. Lap the end of one border over the adjacent border at each corner. With a ruler and pencil, draw a line at an angle from the end of the seam line where the borders are sewn to the quilt top to the outside corner where the two borders cross. Reverse the borders so that the top one is now underneath, and mark a similar line on the other border. Match the lines, pin, and stitch to miter the corner. Trim away the excess fabric from the seam allowance. Repeat this procedure at the other three corners of the quilt.

Finishing 25

Now that your quilt blocks are sewn together and your borders are attached, you are ready for stuffing, lining, quilting or tying, and binding.

Choosing a Quilting Pattern. Small patches are usually just outline quilted 1/4″ in from the seam lines or quilted in the ditch (right along the seam lines). Wide plain borders and sashes, alternate plain blocks, and other large patches are good places to show off fancy quilting. Choose a favorite traditional design for this, or adapt or invent a design of your own. Regroup the elements of the quilting motif to fit patches of different shapes and to fit borders. The quilting design should complement the style of the quilt. Don't use a fussy quilting design for a bold, casual quilt. Contemporary quilts often look good with simple quilting lines that sweep across the entire expanse of the quilt. Traditional-style quilts are lovely with outline quilting supplemented with small detailed florals or other individual motifs in the larger patches.

Marking for Quilting. Outline quilting and quilting in the ditch are done by eye, with no marking necessary. To mark individual quilting motifs in patches or borders, start by tracing the design onto white paper with a black felt pen. Tape the tracing, face up, onto a window or glass table top, and place the quilt top, also face up, over it. Adjust the quilt top to position the motif as desired. Daylight through the window or a lamp placed under the glass table top will help you see the pattern clearly through the fabric. Use a pencil or erasable quilt-marking pen to trace the design onto the fabric. When you have marked each patch and border motif according to your plan, you are ready to stuff, line, and baste the quilt.

Stuffing, Lining, and Basting. Make a lining about 4″ longer and 4″ wider than your quilt top. Unless your quilt is very small or you are using sheeting for lining material, you will have to join two or three lengths of material to make your lining. Trim the selvages off the yard goods before seaming to avoid puckers. Take 1/4″ seams, or take deeper seams and trim to 1/4″. Press the seams open.

Place the lining face down on a large, flat surface such as the floor. Spread the batting evenly over it. If the batting is too small and needs to be spliced, overlap the two batts about three inches. Trim off half of the thickness from each of the two batts where they overlap so that the quilt will be uniformly thick all over. Baste the batting together along the edges where they overlap. Do not stretch the batting as you smooth it over the lining. Trim the excess from the edges.

Next, smooth the quilt top, centered face up, over the lining and batting. Pin. Baste in a large X across the quilt; then baste lines about six inches apart across and down the quilt. Also baste around the edges.

Hand Quilting. Put the quilt in a large frame, basting the excess lining around the edges to the cloth strips of the frame, or use a large hoop to keep the quilt taut. Start quilting in the center, and work your way to the edges. Use a short needle. Make a very small knot in the single strand of thread, insert the needle an inch away, and bring it up at the starting point of your line of quilting. Tug on the thread gently to pull the knot under the surface between the lining and the quilt top. Using a short, even running stitch, quilt through all three layers. At the end of a line of quilting or at the end of your length of thread, take a small back stitch to secure the thread, insert the needle through the top and batting only, bring up the needle an inch or so away from where it entered, and cut the thread right at the surface of the quilt so that it will slip back into the batting. Quilt along the marked lines and around the edges of all patches as planned.

Tying. Tying is a quick alternative to quilting. If you want a very thick comforter that would be difficult to quilt through, tying is the answer. Stuff and line the quilt top as for quilting. Instead of basting, pin through all layers around the edges and at places where you want ties. Block centers and corners are logical places for ties, and you can space ties evenly by eye in these places without measuring. Ties should be no more than about 6″ apart, and a row of ties should be within a couple of inches of the edge of the quilt. To make a tie, thread a fairly large needle with about two yards of lightweight yarn pulled up double. Don't knot it. Insert the needle next to a pin from the front or back, whichever side you choose to have the ties. Remove the pin. Take a stitch about ¼″ long, and bring up the needle. Pull the yarn to within 2″ of the end, tie in a double (square) knot, and cut off the yarn at the needle end even with the tail end. Repeat at each pin.

Binding. A double binding finishes the quilt's edge sturdily. Here is how to make one. Trim the batting and lining even with the quilt top. Cut bias stripping (or straight) 2½″ wide in four pieces just longer than the four sides of the quilt. Fold one of the strips in half lengthwise, with right sides out, lay it over the quilt top with all raw edges even, matching centers, and pin. (The binding strip will extend a little past the quilt at both ends.) Stitch through all layers from end to end with a ¼″ seam. Roll the binding over the edge of the quilt, and pin the folded edge of the binding even with the stitching line. Blind stitch on the back side. Repeat for the opposite side of the quilt. For the remaining two sides, sew only to the seam lines where the first two binding strips are attached. Trim the four strips as necessary, tuck in the ends at an angle to miter the corners, and hand stitch to secure the miters.

A nice finishing touch is to sign and date your quilt in embroidery. You also might like to write down anything of interest about the quilt—the source of the design, any special meaning, anecdotes, or whatever might be significant to the future owner of the quilt.

Further Reading

For good, sound information as well as color photographs, these are my favorite sources.

Bradkin, Cheryl Greider. *The Seminole Patchwork Book.* Atlanta, Georgia: A Yours Truly Publication, 1980. Clear instructions and helpful illustrations on this popular machine-piecing technique. Available from Yours Truly, Box 80218, Atlanta, GA 30366.

Fanning, Robbie and Tony. *The Complete Book of Machine Quilting.* Radnor, Pennsylvania. Chilton Book Company, 1980. Everything you might need to know to understand and enjoy your sewing machine as a tool for piecing, appliqué, or quilting.

James, Michael. *The Quiltmaker's Handbook* and *The Second Quiltmaker's Handbook.* Englewood Cliffs, New Jersey: Prentice-Hall, Inc., 1978/1981. Excellent information on basic and more advanced sewing techniques and quilt design theory and practice. Each volume has a small section devoted to color pictures of exciting contemporary quilts.

Martin, Judy and Leman, Bonnie. *Log Cabin Quilts.* Wheatridge, Colorado: Moon Over the Mountain Publishing Co., 1980. Many color photos of Log Cabin quilts—antique to modern—and complete directions for designing and making quilts from this most versatile pattern. Available from Moon Over the Mountain Publishing Co., 6700 West 44 Ave., Wheatridge, CO 80033.

Orlofsky, Patsy and Myron. *Quilts in America.* New York: Abbeville Press, 1991. Excellent historical information and lovely photos of antique quilts.

Quilter's Newsletter Magazine. Wheatridge, Colorado: Leman Publications, Inc. Published ten times yearly. Chock-full of color pictures, new and traditional quilt patterns, good articles on technique, news, and historical information. Available by subscription or at quilt stores. *Quilter's Newsletter Magazine* is available at Box 394, Wheatridge, CO 80033.

For block or set ideas or color schemes, here are more of my favorites.

Beyer, Jinny. *The Quilter's Album of Blocks and Borders.* McLean, Virginia: EPM Publications, 1986. No color inside but a wealth of unit block drawings and border designs, some original. Carefully drafted and well researched. Available from EPM Publications, Box 490, McLean, VA 22101.

Bishop, Robert. *New Discoveries in American Quilts.* New York: E.P. Dutton, 1975. Contains 192 photos, most in color. Also a good book for historical perspective.

Brackman, Barbara. *An Encyclopedia of Pieced Quilt Patterns.* Lawrence, Kansas: self-published, 1979. Over 3,500 unit block drawings, well researched and organized in a useful format. Available from Ms. Brackman at 500 Louisiana St., Lawrence, KS, 66044.

Gutcheon, Beth. *The Perfect Patchwork Primer.* New York: Viking/Penguin, 1974. A good collection of carefully drafted unit block designs (traditional and original) plus colorful commentary and basic information. Available from Gutcheon Patchworks, 611 Broadway, New York, NY 10012.

Houck, Carter and Miller, Myron. *American Quilts and How to Make Them.* New York: Charles Scribner's Sons, 1975. Forty-two quilts shown, twenty-four in beautiful color, in period settings of the museums and restorations where the quilts are housed.

Martin, Judy and Leman, Bonnie. *Taking the Math Out of Making Patchwork Quilts.* Wheatridge, Colorado: Moon Over the Mountain Publishing Co., 1981. Complete reference book of charts and tables to simplify quilt planning and yardage figuring. Available from Moon Over the Mountain Publishing Co., 6700 West 44 Ave., Wheatridge, CO 80033.

Nelson, Cyril I. *The Quilt Engagement Calendar.* New York: E.P. Dutton, published annually. Contains a full-page color quilt photo for each week of the year. Predominantly antique quilts with a few contemporary ones sprinkled in.

Quiltmaker Magazine. Wheatridge, Colorado: Leman Publications, Inc. Published semiannually. All-new designs in full color, complete patterns and directions. *Quiltmaker* is available through Leman Publications, Wheatridge, CO 80034.

Index of Pattern Names

Pattern name is followed by source and page numbers in this book. Pattern names and sources are from Brackman's *An Encyclopedia of Pieced Quilt Patterns* (see Further Reading). Asterisk (*) indicates pattern is by the author.

KEY TO ABBREVIATIONS

Unit blocks for Color Plates

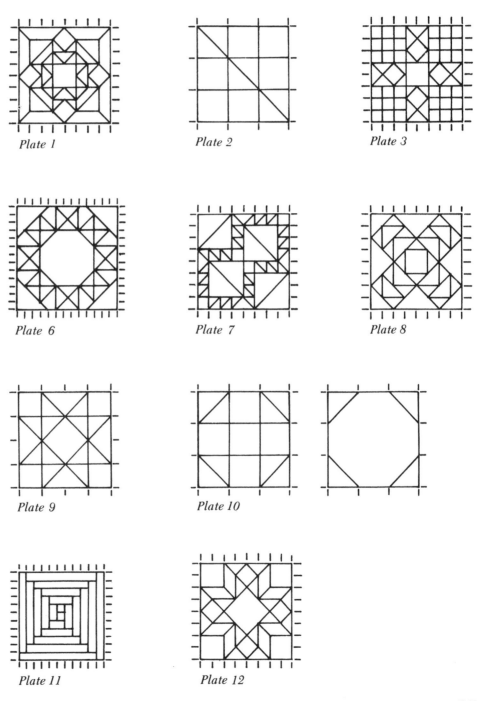

Plate 1

Plate 2

Plate 3

Plate 6

Plate 7

Plate 8

Plate 9

Plate 10

Plate 11

Plate 12

About the Author

Judy Martin grew up in San Diego, the middle of five children of a mother who sewed and a father whose engineering profession encouraged mathematical practicality. She was at home with the sewing machine and with graph paper at an early age. Judy began making quilts when she was a college student at the University of California at Santa Barbara. After graduating with a degree in Social Sciences, she moved to Oregon where she made patchwork comforters to sell at crafts fairs and taught quiltmaking. In 1979 she joined the staff of *Quilter's Newsletter Magazine* as Associate Editor, and she wrote *Log Cabin Quilts* and *Taking the Math Out of Making Patchwork Quilts* with Bonnie Leman. Many of her quilt designs have appeared in *Quilter's Newsletter Magazine* as well as its sister publication, *Quiltmaker.*

Judy lives in Lakewood, Colorado, with her husband, Steve.